Paul H Dunn

ANXIOUSLY ENGAGED

ANXIOUSLY ENGAGED

Paul H. Dunn

Verily I say, men should be anxiously engaged in a good cause, and do many things of their own free will, and bring to pass much righteousness.

—D&C 58:28

Published by
Deseret Book Company
Salt Lake City, Utah
1974

ISBN 0-87747-546-6

Library of Congress Catalog Card No. 74-28591

Lithographed by
DESERET PRESS
in the United States of America

This book is affectionately dedicated to my wonderful children and grandchildren: Janet, Gary, Carolyn; Marsha, Jeril, Tammy, Jeremy; Kellie; and to those yet unborn whose great futures lie ahead. It is their father's and grandfather's great desire and prayer that they always be "anxiously engaged."

Table of Contents

Acknowledgments

Any publication requires the interest and encouragement of others. The author expresses appreciation to his many friends whose lives and experiences have been shared in these pages; to W. James Mortimer and Arlen Grimshaw of Deseret Book for their constant "prodding" and interest; to Eleanor Knowles for her editorial assistance; to my father-in-law, Dr. C. F. Cheverton, for his great insight and shared experiences over the years; and to Sharene Miner, my secretary, for her typing and proofreading.

Particular gratitude is expressed to my wonderful family—to Janet and Gary, to Marsha and Jeril, to Kellie, and to my wife Jeanne—for their usual insight, support, and encouragement.

"He that findeth his life shall lose it: and he that loseth his life for my sake shall find it."

—Matthew 10:39

1

Anxiously Engaged

Many of us claim to be religious. To some a mere belief in a righteous principle is enough. To others it is necessary not only to believe but also to put that belief into action. Religion can be both passive and active.

There is no question what the Lord intended. Note his counsel to his servants:

"For behold, it is not meet that I should command in all things; for he that is compelled in all things, the same is a slothful and not a wise servant; wherefore he receiveth no reward.

"Verily I say, men should be anxiously engaged in a good cause, and do many things of their own free will, and bring to pass much righteousness." (D&C 58:27-28.)

Today we live in a society that seems not to want to be involved. If we are to bring to pass much righteousness, we need to be "doers, not hearers only." Elbert Hubbard once said, "Down in their hearts, wise men know this truth; the only way to help yourself is to help others." "One thing I know," said Albert Schweitzer, "the only ones among you who will be really happy are those who will have sought and found how to serve."

They only echo other counsel of the Lord. "If you would truly find yourself, then lose yourself in serving others." Be "anxiously engaged."

To be anxiously engaged in a very real way is to develop a philosophy of life consistent with the gospel plan. I challenge every reader to analyze his own philosophy as he reads these chapters. Try to determine *how* you would put these basic principles of the gospel to work in your life, and if you will, I promise you, as Descartes did many years ago, "It is not what we take up, but what we give up that makes us rich."

I am never licked until I give up.

2

The Plus Sign

Many years ago while serving in the United States Infantry in the South Pacific, my outfit was making a dry run on a seemingly deserted beach in the Admiralty Islands. When my particular unit went ashore and scattered around on patrol, we came by chance upon a small native village. I will never forget one of the most interesting sights I have ever seen. All of the natives who appeared on the scene had dyed, reddish-orange hair, and every man, woman, and child—in fact, every living creature that I could see: dogs, animals of all sorts—wore a string of large green beads to the end of which were fastened three tiny shells. We learned upon inquiry from a Baptist minister who had labored among these natives that these beaded ornaments were used to ward off the bad results of an "evil eye" and to bring good luck to the person or animal that wore them.

In this strange village so far removed from our own culture, it was believed that bad luck, sometimes even death, would follow if a mere glance from the evil eye of an enemy fell upon a person or animal. Hence, practically all of the animals and people wore such a string of beads.

At the time it recalled to my memory the days when

some of us as kids carried good luck charms or a rabbit's foot in our pockets. Some of us back on the farm were perhaps superstitious enough to hang horseshoes on the barn door or use a hundred and one other symbols to keep off the evil eye of failure or accident. I remember so well the common superstition of all ball players never to step across another player's mitt while it lay on the ground.

Well, I would now like to give you a new "good luck charm," one that is guaranteed to help you throughout your entire life, every month, every day, every hour, protecting you from the bad luck episodes of your life. It is guaranteed to protect your health and make you more likable in your associations with people and more successful in your job. It will insure greater success in your daily work and bring you home to your dwelling place every evening with a sense of "Well done, thou good and faithful servant."

Right now as you read this, wherever you are, picture in your mind a horizontal line crossed by a vertical line. Do you see the picture? Note that it is not a cross but a *plus sign.* It is the sign that protected the life of Colonel Charles Lindbergh on his perilous journey across the ocean after he had previously taken the extra pains to shut himself up in a small sedan and sit at the wheel without rest or sleep for forty-eight hours in order to study the effects upon himself of confinement, vibration, and motor lullaby; the sign that brought popularity and wealth to all of the great athletes, musicians, scientists, novelists, and business executives of this great country who, after many efforts, finally succeeded.

Scientists have said that the average person uses only about 1/100 of the capacity that God has given him. We know that 1 + 1 = 2, and 5 + 5 = 10—but it takes the plus sign to do the trick. Extra hope for those of us who are discouraged, who sometimes get down in the dumps—a little added patience and determination when all seems lost—may turn the advancing army of decay and start the forward march that leads to victory and our abounding triumph as a person in life, as a leader, as a student, or whatever our calling may be.

And if there is one single person, man, woman, or young person, who is discouraged because of failure, seemingly on his part, to attain his ideals or some special goal, and who is just about ready to give up because of continued loss and discouragement, let him or her remember, as Elbert Hubbard has told us, that the line between failure and success is so fine that often a single extra effort is all that is needed to bring victory out of apparent defeat. History tells us that George Washington lost nine consecutive battles, but by adding the tenth, he won the war and the liberty of our country. F. W. Woolworth made a failure of his first three stores, but the plus sign of the fourth did the trick. Henry Ford was once asked, "What would you do if you lost everything you had?" "Give me ten years," he said, "and I would build it all back again."

We might well ask, Why do I have so many problems? Why is life always such a struggle? I seem to have more bad days than good days. The plan of salvation as given by our Lord and Savior, Jesus Christ, was intended to build our spiritual strength and character through trials and hardships. It's the sweet reward of adversity.

As a young woman of eighteen, a pretty model found her dreams shattered by an automobile accident that confined her to a wheelchair with partially paralyzed legs. Because of the accident, she learned to play the piano. Because of the accident, she learned to develop a sense of humor and to find that there is a funny viewpoint to almost any subject. And in time her legs regained their strength, and she became an actress gifted with a sense of humor that made her one of the outstanding comediennes of our day. You have heard her on the radio and you have seen her in motion pictures and particularly on television, and you know that Lucille Ball was not stopped by adversity. On the contrary, it was the plus sign that made her grow in stature.

Randolph Eyre tells the story about the town of Enterprise, Alabama, which has raised a monument in honor of the boll weevil, the dreaded insect pest of the cotton country that once threatened to ruin this important crop. You would naturally wonder why anyone would want to erect a monument to a pest. Then you discover that it is because the inroads against and destruction of the boll weevil resulted in the planting of other crops—and that the sweet potato and the peanut, in particular, have been of vast importance to the South.

The diversification of crops made the South versatile. The people learned that everything did not hinge on cotton—and rise or fall with it. This meant a more stable and prosperous economy. In other words, an enemy did the South a good turn. The bad break became a good one. The bad luck turned to good luck. Hardships, trials, and tribulations have their place in the great plan of life.

And so I say, whatever the battle in which we are engaged—and no doubt all of us have some difficulties to face—better than all the beads, seashells, and buckeyes, horseshoes, and other modern charms is the armor on which is painted, with our own life's blood, the plus sign, meaning that with each crushed hope there is another hope and stronger faith; with each fall in the road, another trial.

Someone has said, "I am never licked until I give up." And the author of one of our sacred books tells us that to him who overcometh (and it doesn't matter where he started in life's race) shall be given the crown of life. It is the plus sign, the sign that points always forward and upward, not backward, the sign that recognizes defeat only as an opportunity for further effort in the future. By this sign we shall conquer.

". . . choose you this day whom ye will serve"

—Joshua 24:15

3

What Is Courage?

While fighting in the Pacific during World War II, I witnessed pain and death many times. Each time, just before going to battle, the soldiers were terribly frightened, and many expressed the feeling that they were afraid they were going to die. These experiences frequently brought to my mind one of Shakespeare's oft-quoted lines of poetry: "Cowards die many times before their deaths; the valiant never taste of death but once." (*Julius Caesar,* Act. 2, scene 2.)

Courage has different forms. Sometimes it is a man facing a very difficult situation, such as a battle line in time of war; sometimes it is an everyday thing—a man doing his job as a policeman or business executive. The work is hard, and it is there every day; there is no glamour, but there is always a challenge. The brave men in these cases are the ones who get the job done—every day.

There are courageous men in all walks of life, just as in each profession there are also the quitters. There aren't too many of them, because they don't last—they give in to the problems they face. Things look too big or too tough or as though they will take too much time. The quitters do not work hard enough. The man who is good is the man who works hard at it; who sticks with the difficult thing, works at it, and finally wins out.

Someone has said, "Bravery is a complicated thing to describe." It cannot be measured nor identified by color, nor does it have an odor. It is a quality, not a thing. One of the most widely quoted definitions of courage is the famous one of Ernest Hemingway: "Guts," he said, "is grace under pressure." In other words, courage is doing what you have to do in a tough spot, and doing it calmly.

A true story told by Mickey Mantle will help to illustrate: During the battle of Leyte in the Philippine Islands in World War II, an army sergeant led a squad of twelve infantry soldiers through some very dense jungle toward an enemy pillbox. As the Americans came out of the woods and made their way toward the fortress, it was quiet, and they did not expect any trouble, but suddenly there was a burst of enemy machine-gun fire from the dugout. It was what American soldiers call an ambu gun, which fired 700 rounds (bullets) per minute. I mention this only to show that the American soldiers knew at once that it was enemy fire.

At the instant my friend heard the ambu-gun fire, he dove flat on the ground, half in and half out of a muddy pond, but with his eyes constantly on the target. For a moment all of the men in the patrol who observed the action thought their sergeant had been hit. Knowing that he was trapped directly in front of the pillbox, the other soldiers quickly took cover. Then, before they could realize just what had happened, their leader was up on his knees, firing his rifle into the narrow slits of the pillbox. Within a moment he had achieved his objective.

What had happened was this: The sergeant had heard the ambu gun and dropped immediately on his face, which was instinctive; at the same time he reacted as the leader of the patrol and did what he had to do. He was not wounded, and he did not go all the way down on his face to hide, as all the men behind him instinctively did. He knew at once that he could not stay face down on the ground because the enemy would pick off his entire patrol one by one. So he dropped only momentarily, rolled over, got to his knees, swung his rifle into firing position, and fought back. The action was soon over, and the Americans had won. What the sergeant did took courage—"grace under pressure."

Courage does not have to happen only in war. Being brave does not mean you have to be big and noisy. It means doing what you have to do even when you do not want to do it, or when it is hard to do, or when you could let the job slide and watch somebody else do it. Being courageous covers a lot of ground. Shakespeare called it being valiant. There are a lot of other words that could be substituted for valiant: bravery, courage, spirit, backbone, fortitude, heart. If you read about a soldier climbing out of a foxhole and braving enemy fire to reach a wounded companion and carrying him back to safety, it sounds right to call this courage or bravery. But take an ordinary situation in an ordinary life: Have you ever had the experience of standing before a large congregation? How did you feel? Were you scared? Of course you were. Who isn't?

Several years ago, in my youth, I came to know personally the great baseball player Lou Gehrig. Because of my admiration and respect for this man, I asked him one day how I might overcome my fear and anxiety as a competitor on the ball field. Without hesitation, he said, "Paul, don't ever lose your fear; just learn to control it. Fear is a wonderful asset because it keeps a person humble and reminds him that he can't accomplish his objective alone. There is a higher source than man, and each time I go to perform I call upon that Divine Power for assistance."

Then he added, "Fear also reminds me that there are eight other players on the team, and their strength is my strength."

It takes team effort to succeed. Gehrig pointed out

further that we can learn to control our fears by discovering our individual strengths and then applying these strengths in the areas of our limitations.

Perhaps you have had the experience of being the only person in a crowd who believed in the principles of the gospel. There is no pressure quite like the pressure that can be brought to bear when the peer group would have us do that which is contrary to our basic beliefs. For example: Members of your group of friends have the habit of taking the name of the Lord in vain. Because you don't, they make you feel that you are the one who is peculiar. It takes as much strength and courage to stand up against this kind of pressure, and ofttimes ridicule, as it does for the athlete or soldier to perform his feats of heroism.

It took the same kind of courage and strength for men like Joshua and Gideon to accomplish the things the Lord asked them to do. Each day of our lives we find it necessary to remember Joshua's admonition: ". . . choose you this day whom ye will serve." (Joshua 24:15.) To stand up and be counted, whether it is in the time of Joshua, on a battlefield, or in a social situation at school, faith and courage are required.

As a young lad, Gideon lacked self-confidence. In humility he had said that he was one of the least important of his father's family. It took a lot of persuading and a great deal of inspiration to make him brave enough to attack his job, but when he was convinced that the Lord really wanted him to lead the people and drive out the enemy, he measured up in a fine way. He had no fear of his townsmen when he tore down their altar to the pagan god Baal. He was fired with courage when he assembled his army. He was filled with daring when, with a small band of only three hundred men, he defeated the hosts of the Midianites and liberated his people from bondage.

Almost without exception, great leaders in all ages have been humble men who, through faith and courage, have become instruments in the hands of God. Often success comes easily to those with great abilities and talents, and when it does, bad habits of laziness and indifference come as easily. Too often, before the goal is attained, such people become defeated and destroyed by their own talents. Hard work, faith, and courage make us strong and help us overcome our obstacles. It does not matter how many talents we have; what matters is how we use them.

Time: "the most precious of all possessions"

—Benjamin Franklin

4

On Time

Have you thought of this inconsistency of American life—that everybody is always in a hurry, yet few people ever get any place on time, except, of course, to meet certain compulsory appointments? And has it occurred to you also that this very fact offers a wide-open opportunity for one who is prompt to gain a favorable position in the eyes of his fellowmen?

If we were living in a place where railway trains stopped along the way for engineers to hunt rabbits, if we had no interurban cars to catch, no banquets, theaters, or meetings to attend—if we were not pulled by a multitude of demands that make swift action so necessary—perhaps it wouldn't matter. But in the midst of such a swiftly moving society, the one who receives our recognition and gains our favor is the one who, by his promptness and dependability, makes it easier for us to keep in motion.

I remember reading of an old man who had lived to be ninety years of age, and during that time he said he had spent thirty years waiting for other people. I suspect that most of us who are not nearly so aged feel like saying much the same thing. True, we joke about it and laugh at the people who always come late, but the fact remains that beneath that smile is deep respect for the man or woman who, when he promises to be present at a certain time, will be present at that time he committed, and not a moment later.

But there is another and bigger reason for being on time. Horace Mann, one of our early educators, said, "Unfaithfulness in keeping an appointment is an act of clear dishonesty. He may as well borrow a person's money as his time." And when you borrow one's time you are taking, as Benjamin Franklin would say, "the most precious of all possessions, something which when lost can never be found, when taken away can never be returned."

How many times I have seen a college teacher in his classroom with thirty students before him: the bell has rung, the roll has been taken, and the teacher and students have reached a point of definite interest of their discussion. Then suddenly the door opens and in walks a tardy student. The eyes of all members of the class are turned in his direction, the teacher pauses in his discussion, and for at least sixty seconds the work, or at least the attention of the group, is suspended—one moment for each of thirty students and one professor, or a total of more than half an hour of valuable time wasted for the class as a whole by the tardiness of one student. I have also seen a classroom lecture, Sunday School class, or public address practically ruined by the staggering in of tardy people at the wrong moment.

What shall we say of these people as well as others who carelessly keep others in a group or public gathering waiting for twenty or thirty minutes? Are they criminals? No, we can hardly call them that. Thieves? Perhaps that also is too strong a term for folks who do not realize the inconvenience and waste that they are causing. But certainly we are justified in asking such people to read and reread and say to themselves with Horace Mann, "Unfaithfulness in keeping an appointment is an act of clear dishonesty. He may as well borrow a person's money as his time." And again, we can say with Benjamin Franklin: "If time be of all things most precious, wasting time must be the greatest prodigality, since lost time is never found again."

If I could somehow summon all of the leading business and professional men and women of this nation and ask them to speak to the young people who are interested in achieving something worthwhile in a vocation, I am sure they would include among the first principles the following commitments: "Be prompt in keeping appointments. Be prompt in the payment of your bills. Be prompt in the accomplishment of any task that is committed to you." And I venture to hope that at least for this one day not one of us will want to waste a moment of another's time. It may be more precious to him than silver or gold!

"And whosoever will be chief among you, let him be your servant."

—Matthew 20:27

5

Buttons and Ties

I had an experience some time ago that every man, and I suppose every boy, has had at one time or another in his life. I was dressing in preparation for going to work and had about completed the task when I discovered that my only clean white shirt had the collar button missing. Everything else was ready—shoes shined, clothes pressed, hair combed, even my necktie was selected. But by its absence, one tiny missing button slowed up the whole program of the day.

Well, in time the button was sewn back in place and all was right again. The experience, however, taught me a lesson. I had been disturbed because with all the time and preparation I had put into getting dressed and ready, and with a great selection of ties to choose from, I was completely dependent upon one little collar button.

So the world is disturbed too, and greatly hindered in its work, because there are too many human neckties—too many people who want to show off in the front of the crowd and too few who want to work in the background where they give of themselves to some worthy cause without any desire for credit.

A case in point: A young priesthood holder sixteen years old, a popular boy, good athlete, fine student, and semiactive in his quorum, was selected president of his group. Upon hearing the news, one of the regular attenders asked one of his classmates about the reason. His friend replied, "Well, he's a good fellow but he hardly ever comes to church. We thought if he were named class president, he would come." And sure enough, as long as he held the position of prominence, he was present and on time, and he even showed some enthusiasm. But just as soon as he was released from office, he sank back into his old habits.

Did you ever hear of such a thing in politics? Every president of a club, every leader, every chairman of a committee from the beginning of time has learned sooner or later that it is easier to persuade people to work for glory than at some task of equal or greater importance where the personal credit is small.

Since there are so many neckties in the world and so few collar buttons at hand—since so many people refuse to serve except in positions of honor—your chance and mine at winning confidence and power in business, school, and the social world becomes all the easier. By simply making ourselves inconspicuous and our functions primary in our thoughts and actions, surrendering ourselves so completely to our task, we can become silently—yet eloquently—so indispensable to those above or about us that none can really fill our place.

As one writer has said, "If you have a boss, boss him." Imagine an intelligent, full-grown man—one who owns a perfectly good pair of shoes, a good suit, a nice-looking necktie—being bossed, disturbed, and held up in his work by a tiny button. But it can be done, because the button can prove itself in a very quiet, but humble, way indispensable to the one who owns it.

If you have sufficient poetic ability, change these words: "If you can't be a pine on top of the hill, be a shrub in the valley." Then put in their place some words like these: "If you can't be the flashiest tie in the front of a collar, be the best little button underneath."

In reality, it is not really a surprising principle after all. The greatest of all teachers, our Lord and Savior, was an example of the ultimate standard of successful living. He said, "And whosoever will be chief among you, let him be your servant: Even as the Son of man came not to be ministered unto, but to minister. . . ." (Matthew 20:27-28.)

"Tiny bits of power properly directed"

—C. F. Cheverton

6

Little Gas-Much Power

Have you ever noticed how many times a teacher makes a significant statement without ever knowing it? I remember one day riding in a car with a very distinguished leader and teacher, returning from a trip where we had been together. As the car rolled along smoothly at about fifty miles an hour, my friend was saying, "What a wonderful thing the automobile is. We turn the key, hold the steering wheel, and glide along at the speed we choose to almost any place we want to go—the result of small explosions from a few drops of gas." Then came his significant remark: "It's all the result of tiny bits of power properly directed."

A heavy car carrying several people is easily moved; great trucks with tons of weight, the engines that build our dams and powerhouses, mighty factories where goods are made to clothe and feed the world, all are propelled by tiny bits of power properly directed.

I recall hearing a scientist say that at present we are only using a fraction of the great power that is in a gallon of gas, and that in a spoonful of water there is sufficient power, when we learn how to use it, to drive a gigantic ocean vessel across the ocean. We do not need to find more power; we need only to learn how to properly direct what we already have.

Have you ever stopped to think that the same thing is true with our human machines? The trouble with so many people who fail is not that they are lacking in power or ability, but that the power they have is not sufficiently organized and directed.

"You have the ability to become an outstanding musician," a teacher once said to one of her students. But the student is still no further along than she was ten years ago.

On the other hand, I recall a young man in Los Angeles who wanted to be an operatic star. Several teachers told him that it would do him no good to try because, they said, "you just don't have the voice." But unwilling to give up, he finally discovered one teacher who saw the value of his hidden talent and big determination. Today, after years of conscientious, careful direction of his power toward a single goal, he is one of the most pleasing and highly honored singers on the West Coast.

Did you know that Verdi, the composer of some of our finest grand operas, was at one time refused admission to a music conservatory because of his apparent lack of natural ability; and that a prominent music teacher once refused to take Caruso as a student because he could see in Caruso's voice no promise in the musical world?

Just recently I spoke with a great surgeon who has the reputation of having some of the clearest brains of any person living in the world. When I asked how he achieved such a high degree of intelligence, he replied, "By the same process that made Hank Aaron a great baseball player. As a child I displayed no more than average intelligence, but I gave up everything that I thought would hinder my physical and mental process and focused my energies constantly on the task of a perfect physical and mental development. What I have done," says this great physician, "many others could do if they were willing, as I have been, to direct their talent completely toward a definite goal."

And so it goes. Most of us know of many cases of particular individuals who years ago were just average or less but who were not satisfied with mediocrity or the average, and who today exhibit great personal talent. By aligning themselves with great causes, seeking out people who are geniuses in their field, and training and disciplining themselves, they have gone on to make tremendous contributions to themselves and to society.

Anyone who has ever worked with young people and followed them through a period of years knows that it isn't the amount of talent with which they start any more than it is the volume of gas that is poured into an automobile that determines the uphill climb; rather, it is the way in which the little or the much is directed and controlled. The more gas, the more danger if it is not properly used. The more natural ability, the greater the calamity if it is not wisely controlled. Ask the wardens of our penitentiaries and the managers of our asylums if that is not true.

Given an average grade of intelligence, wise direction, and willingness to pay the price of concentrated and consecrated effort—not once a week but constantly, every day of every year—we will find that the secrets of life have a way of yielding themselves beyond our fondest dreams.

". . . let your communication be,
Yea, yea; Nay, nay. . ."

—Matthew 5:37

7

Honesty

"I cross my heart and hope to die." Did you ever make that pledge as a youngster? That's what we used to say, as kids, to convince another that we were telling the truth. In ancient Palestine the people had another custom. When one was anxious to prove his honesty, he said to another, "I swear by heaven that I speak the truth," or "I swear by the earth" or "by the hair of my head," or by any number of things that were held especially sacred. The Savior himself, seeing this custom and realizing how impossible it was to build a successful life or a prosperous nation on any such slipshod principle, said that the thing to do was not to prove our honesty by oaths, but to be so truthful that oaths would not be necessary to substantiate our word.

". . . let your communication be, Yea, yea; Nay, nay," he said. (Matthew 5:37.) Be so truthful and so above suspicion in all that you speak or do that when you say "yes," men know that "yes" is right, and when you say "no," they can be assured that "no" is correct.

What would happen if this principle of honesty were practiced by everyone in our country or, for that matter, the world? (Don't think I'm foolish enough to believe that it will be practiced in the near future, but what would happen if it were?)

In the first place, I contend that it would cost us less for crime and the work of our courts. Think of almost any big trial in which the government has prosecuted a criminal, and remember that many thousands of dollars have been spent by the government to gain a few facts which might have been had in five minutes of time had we known for certain that the defendant was telling the truth. When you think of the numerous, long-extended trials of this nature that must be conducted every year in this country, you will realize the awful waste of money and time and effort on the part of our government in its attempt to find the truth that people cannot be depended upon to tell.

But worse than this is the unstable condition produced in society by the practice of dishonesty. I remember an incident that occurred in my life as a teenager. One day a friend of mine lied to his father, in my presence, about taking out the family car. When I challenged him about this, he said, "Oh, that's all right. You see, I did it because I did not want to hurt my father's feelings." Thoughtful, yes, but an act that made it impossible for me to ever know whether he was telling me the truth or was lying for the sake of my feelings. Even I, as a teenager, could tell the difference.

As long as the act of dishonesty is prevalent in a nation, suspicion falls upon us. Conscientious physicians must pay the price of having thrown at them such unfair jokes as, "Did you really need an operation, or did your doctor need a car?" Honest lawyers—of which there are so many in the land—are often discounted because of the false practices of others among their group; and we peddle the joke about "Since you won your case, I suppose you'll take your trip to Europe?" "No, my lawyer will make it for me."

Politician, huh? The very name brands the best of

men before they can have a chance to prove their sincerity of purpose. It is not hard for the world to classify religious people as hypocrites, philanthropists as publicity seekers, capitalists as grinders of the poor, and miners as ignorant strikers.

There is no end to such unjust classifications, and unfair as these suspicions may be, they will continue as long as there is the practice of dishonesty by some persons in these groups, for as a great educator once said, "Dishonesty counterfeits the circulating medium of society." As long as there is any considerable amount of counterfeit money, we may be suspicious of every real bill or coin we have. As long as there is dishonest, counterfeit speech, it is only natural that the speech and actions of all of us will be held in question until they are proved to be of honest weight.

Honesty on the part of all in a nation would mean economic and social stability, fairness, freedom from suspicion, and a dependable "circulating medium of society." Would it not be worth a trial?

". . . faith, if it hath not works, is dead . . ."

—James 2:17

8

Our Actions Speak

Some time ago while sitting in a sacrament meeting, I heard an older missionary couple relate this story. They said that while visiting a certain family in a far-off country, they heard about a family that had been stricken with much poverty. These missionaries prayed with some of the leaders of the local branch, and as they were upon their knees one day, one of the leaders prayed earnestly that God would help these poverty-stricken neighbors before they starved to death. At the close of the prayer the man's little daughter came in and asked, "Dad, why do you bother God with a matter that you can take care of yourself?"

"Humph!" he thought. "Bother God with a matter that you can take care of yourself!" Such a preposterous idea had not entered his head before, because he had been thinking of religion as a definition to be accepted rather than a life to be lived. He had believed—or thought he had—in God the Father; he said he believed in Christ; he said he believed in the scriptures; he said he believed in the Church; he said he believed in prayer and in the theory of love. And he had fooled himself into thinking that this system of beliefs, which he could write down and perhaps even frame upon the wall of his mind, constituted religion itself.

It took his practical-minded, sincere young daughter to show him what the apostle James had taught two thousand years ago—that no matter how much theoretical faith a person has, if it does not cause him to behave differently from the person who has no faith, it is proof that he has none either. "Faith without works is dead," which means that unless you do something about what you think you believe, it is a sign that you do not really believe it.

I remember once seeing a movie in which a picture that was hanging on a wall began, at an appointed time, to move. Then slowly but surely a figure stepped out of the picture frame and began to walk about and take its place in the activities of the people in the room. I have often wondered what would happen if a person's faith or belief could step down from a wall and, taking hold of its owner's arm, say, "Come on, brother, we're going out to *do* what you say every day that you believe." Would there be some stammering and side-stepping in a lot of cases?

"You tell me," says the person's belief, as it ushers us out the door, "that you believe in God as the Father of all mankind. All right, let's go out and see how the rest of the great family of our Heavenly Father is getting along. There may be need for us to miss our dinner and give up a proposed entertainment, but one can always make sacrifices when members of the family are in need of our help. Now don't begin making excuses and drawing back. If you do, I won't go back upon the wall of your home again.

"For the last ten years you have said that you believe in the Church and its teachings. Yet I saw you really skimp as you made out your tithing and fast offering last Sunday and spent during the week many times that for some pleasure. You spent over fifteen dollars for a night at the football game and several more dollars for the gas and oil necessary to enjoy a wonderful ride in your family car last week.

"Now don't begin to make excuses," your creed continues. "It is your right to have some fun, but that small amount you wrote last week for the great work accomplished by the church which you claim to love with all your heart, and the seven or eight dollars or more you spent in trivialities, do not bear out your advertised claims."

If our true beliefs could talk in such a fashion—if they could step down from the walls of our home or the walls of our mind and say "I will not go back until you have proved by your works that you really believe in me"—how much of a belief would we have left at the end of the day?

Well, whether we'd like to admit it or not, and however much we may fool our own consciences, in the eyes of the Lord and before the people who know us best, the only true faith is the one that we prove in our daily lives. What a joke it must be to people who watch us carefully, both in and out of the Church, to hear some of us make loud confessions of faith in God and love for our brethren and then see us prove by our actions during the week that we don't believe a thing we say.

"But what shall I do if my faith is dead?" you ask.

Begin to act as though it were alive. Then strangely enough, in most cases it will be revived. Even as real faith cannot exist without leading to good works, so good works cannot continue long without giving strength to faith. The two go hand-in-hand. If we have one, it is generally not hard to secure the other.

"Control thyself."

—Cicero

9

Self-Control

I witnessed a very funny thing some time ago. I suppose I should not have smiled at it, but it was certainly funny. A man had vowed, in the presence of many of us, that he would not commit another sin as long as he lived; he said he had made a lot of mistakes in the past, but from that time on he was going to exercise perfect self-control. Someone in the group joked with him about his resolution, and at that he became so angry he wanted to pick a fight.

He would never make another mistake, huh? I guess the poor fellow didn't realize that the ability to control oneself in the time of temptation can be developed only after much painstaking practice. Sometimes we all have to work different kinds of tricks on ourselves to hold our emotions in check, but an energetic person works hard and studies several hours a day to develop other types of ability. Why is it not also worth practice to gain control over one's emotions? I believe that it is, but I'm quite sure from my own experience that it's no easy job. Suppose we look at some of the plans that others have found helpful.

The late Colonel Charles Lindbergh, when asked

what method he used, said that he concluded that if he knew the difference between the right way to do a thing and the wrong way to do it, it was up to him to train himself to do the right thing at all times. So he drew up a list of characteristics that he wished to develop and listed them on the left side of a sheet of paper. Then each evening he would read off his entire list. After those characteristics that he felt he had developed to some extent during the day, he would place a little red cross, and after those character factors that he felt he had violated during the day, he would draw a black cross. Those that he had not been called upon to demonstrate that day would receive no mark. After checking himself this way over a period of time, he would compare the number of red and black crosses and see whether he was getting better or worse. He said that he was generally glad to note improvement as he grew older. Altogether he had listed fifty-eight character factors, among which were altruism, calmness in temper, clean speech, justice, modesty, virtue, no sarcasm, and punctuality.

Another method that one of our leaders has used successfully is to write each desirable characteristic on a separate card, classifying them so there will be as many cards as there are days in the month. For example, perhaps on the first card he has written "sincerity." Today that card will be looked at the first thing in the morning and placed in his pocket. And although he tries every day to be sincere, on this day he will take particular pains to keep this characteristic in mind and to practice it. Tomorrow another card is used, and so on until an entire month is past and each of these wholesome characteristics has held for one day a special place in the thoughts and actions of the owner. Then the plan is carried out in the following months with the same group of cards. Now I suspect that such a scheme would not work advantageously with all, but this leader declares that he has found it to be very helpful to him and to many other persons.

Others notice considerable development in character

by picking some one person who has achieved an extraordinary degree of moral strength and then judging all his actions by the life of this ideal. Have I been as kind in all my dealings this day as he would have been? If not, then I need to be more careful tomorrow. Do I have as perfect control of my temper as he does? Am I as sympathetic? Do I go out of my way as much as he to help the one in trouble? Only when we can say yes to such questions may we be satisfied with our accomplishment of self-control. And if we pick some personality to emulate who is sufficiently perfect, we shall no doubt be struggling upward to the end of our lives.

Many of our prophets have laid emphasis upon the value of selecting Jesus Christ as an ideal and trying in every activity of the day to do as he would do if he were here in the flesh today. One senses the difficulty in knowing in every case just what Jesus would do, yet in the face of this challenge, I have a feeling that in our very attempt to catch his spirit and follow his example—the example of the greatest personality of all time—we will find constant stimulus to higher and better living than at present.

As one author has said, "After Him there is nothing more but to develop and fructify. Whatever may be the surprises of the future, Jesus will never be surpassed. All ages will proclaim that among the sons of man there is none greater than Jesus."

Napoleon said, "From first to last, Jesus is the same, always the same—majestic and simple, infinitely severe yet infinitely gentle. Everything in Him amazes me—His progress through all centuries and kingdoms—all this to me, a progeny, an unfathomable mystery. I defy you to cite any other life like that of Christ's."

And then we remember the memorable words of Jean Paul Richter: "He is the mightiest among the holy, and the holiest among the mighty. He has with his pierced hands lifted empires off their hinges, turned the stream of centuries out of its channels, and still rules the ages."

I am convinced that regardless of the technique that

we may employ in the development of better habits, there is no pattern so perfect nor no source of inspiration so helpful as that of our Savior, who, being born under humble circumstances and reared in the little country of Palestine, became the Master of all, Jesus the Christ, the Son of God.

"When I was a child, I spake as a child, I understood as a child, I thought as a child: but when I became a man, I put away childish things."

—1 Corinthians 13:11

10

Human Earthquakes

Those who live on the West Coast of the United States and in other parts of South America and the Pacific know for a certainty, through practical experience, the damage done by earthquakes. An earthquake does for a city much the same as an outburst of temper does for an individual. Both are destructive. Both ruin appearances. Both are liable to leave terrible memories that can never be forgotten. Both are similar in that we seldom know when either is coming. Nevertheless, we prepare for earthquakes in every way that we know. The very fact that we do not know the time of coming makes it all the more necessary to prepare well for such an emergency. Would it not be wise also to lay foundations to withstand the strain of temper and also to devise plans for escaping its more serious results!

Scientists have conducted experiments to learn the result of anger on digestion. In one such experiment, after a hungry dog had been tied in a room, a cat was brought in, causing the dog to become greatly excited. The cat was then removed, and the dog was given food to eat, with the result that almost no gastric juice was secreted. Another time, after the dog had begun to eat and the gastric juices had started to flow, the cat was brought in, and the gastric juices almost entirely stopped flowing.

So it is with temper and rage; they check the secretion of all the juices that are essential to the chemical changes in food during digestion, say our scientists. And for some time after a fit of anger, digestion ceases in human beings as well as in the lower forms of animals. So violent indeed is the effect of anger on the human body that it sometimes cause strokes or sudden death. Does it not seem rather strange that some folks can be sufficiently concerned about their health to pay attention to exercise, food, and rest, and then give way to violent anger?

One of my friends once said, "If you're going to get rid of temper, you must give it a chance to explode without hurting anybody."

"How do you do this?" I asked.

"You'd be surprised," he said, "and you may laugh, but it works. When I become so angry I can't hold the anger in any longer, I go someplace where no one can see or hear me and holler just as loud as I can." A strange method, but his principle is sound, using his heated energy in some definite way.

I remember once telling a hot-headed athlete on a ball team of which I was a member to try whistling whenever he lost his temper. I was on the road for several weeks before I saw him again, and when I came back home, I asked how he had gotten along. "Oh," he said, "it worked beautifully. I was whistling about three-fourths of the time, but we won more games."

One man tells me that when he is tempted to become angry with people, he always reminds himself that his enemy of the moment has two parts to his nature (as every person has two parts): what might be called, in mathematical terms, the common denominator and the numerator. "All of us," he says to himself, "are human beings, brothers and sisters, and therefore have much in common. But each of us has different numerators, peculiarities, that are different from those of every other person. When I get disgusted with the other fellow's peculiarities of belief and action, speaking again mathematically, I try to remind myself that while his numerator may be different from mine, we have a common denominator—we are still brothers. I can't hate a brother."

Another of my friends adds to this statement that we are also tied up in a vital way with one great universe: each of us is so much a part of Heavenly Father's concern that one cannot become angry with another without injuring the heart of our Father.

Another says, "It helps me to control myself when I realize what a childish thing it is to become violently angry. Babies cry when they can't get their milk. Boys fuss and fight when they cannot have their way on a baseball field or in almost any activity of life. But I am not a baby that must have his bottle every time he wants it. My mind can see further than a six-month-old child. I can reason better than a teenage boy. I have ideas, judgment, ideals, hopes, aspirations, and loves that belong only to the mature person. In every other respect, I am a full-grown man. Shall I remain a child in respect only to the control of my temper?"

Old Testament writers, New Testament teachers, other religious leaders, and the principles of successful business and good sportsmanship all tell us, "Control yourself—keep your head—be patient." In the words of the apostle Paul, "When I was a child, I spake as a child, I understood as a child, I thought as a child: but when I became a man, I put away childish things." (1 Corinthians 13:11.)

Another says, "I may get terribly excited and lose my temper, but I never allow myself to make an important decision of any kind until the spell has passed, and I never write an important letter until at least the next day."

Now, it may be that none of the schemes mentioned

here will help you personally. I hope they may. Perhaps the most important thing is to realize the great importance of finding some method to control our tempers, since bursts of temper are really destructive to individual personality even as earthquakes are to a city.

"We disagree with our heads, but we're pals at heart."

11

Barbershop Philosophy

If you want to learn the latest news and the choicest gossip, don't read the newspapers; go to a barbershop. One may learn some pretty good lessons there also as he studies and compares the various types of people who come and go.

I remember an experience I had some time ago that I feel is worth passing on. As I entered the door of the barbershop, I found the room empty except for two barbers, who were arguing rapidly and loudly about some political issue. At first I thought they were about to come to blows, but as I seated myself in the chair of one of the barbers, the other laughed and told a funny story that completely changed the atmosphere and gave to all of us the spirit of good cheer.

"You're a couple of funny fellows," I said to the one who was cutting my hair. "One moment you're at sword's point and the next moment you're acting like the best of friends."

"Oh, we weren't angry at each other," he said. "We were just shooting off our heads." Did you get that remark? It is very significant. "We were just shooting off our heads," he repeated, "but we never fight, because we're buddies at heart. We disagree with our heads, but we're pals at heart."

And I thought: Here at last is the solution to our problems—in the family, in the church, in politics, in industry, in the majority, if not in all, of our vexing social problems.

Two principles are involved here. The first is our open and above-board recognition of the fact that in our heads, we are different, and we always will be as long as life lasts. Mother Nature is sufficiently fastidious to want no two specimens alike. This reminds me of a story I heard once several years ago in the military. It seems that two Englishmen, two Irishmen, and two Americans were shipwrecked and left to make their way together on a distant island. Later, after they had been found and their diaries examined, it was noted that the Irishmen had fought twice a day, the Englishmen had refused to speak to each other because they had not been introduced, and the Americans had started a drugstore and a Rotary Club.

A second principle in the solution of social problems suggested by my experience with the two barbers is the sympathetic recognition of the fundamental likeness of humanity at heart—all of us differing in our heads, with as many interpretations of life as there are people in the world, but at heart we are primarily the same. According to psychologists, man is by nature a social being. He is not a Democrat or a Republican by nature; he's not a Latter-day Saint, a Presbyterian, a Catholic, or a Baptist by nature; he is not a believer in this or that theory of home life by nature. Man is by nature a social being.

Many true stories are told to us by our returning missionaries that show the wonderful transformations in the lives of people of many different cultures when they are converted to the gospel, not as a result of argument, but through the sharing of the simple gospel truths of brotherly love.

To try to bring peace among the members of a family by attempting to argue every point into perfect agreement, or to endeavor to reconcile capital and labor or politics of opposite sides by a cold-blooded conference and debate, is like attempting to collect all the water of the seas into a single bucket and locking it up for safe keeping.

Nature has a better way. Two barbers could argue politics and religion from morning till night and yet be happy together, because they were buddies at heart. Individual differences seen through the eye of the mind are still individual differences filled with the potentiality of misunderstanding and trouble; but seen through the prism of a sympathetic heart couched in the spirit of the gospel, they are like the different colors of the rainbow: unlike, but necessary for a varied and beautiful world.

Before this day is over, divided families could be united, political enemies could become friends, and most of our social problems would be on the way to a peaceful solution, if only we could agree to disagree—if only we could differ with our heads and be pals at heart.

"Give me a great thought."

—Schiller

12

Tickets, Please

A big, slouchy drunk sat peacefully sleeping one night on the front row of a Salvation Army gospel meeting. In his better days, the man had been a barker in a circus—you know, one of those loud fellows who stands out in front of a sideshow trying to entice people to go inside.

On this particular night, he was oblivious to all his surroundings, peacefully snoozing, until there came a sudden bang on the gospel drum, whereupon he jumped guiltily to his feet and hollered out, "Ladies and gentlemen, right after the big show is over, our gentlemanly ushers will pass among you with tickets to see our after-concert elegant and beautiful girls, funny comedians, and Dr. Mandrake, the mystifying magician. Tickets only 50¢," and so on until he finally came to himself and realized where he was.

I wish I could tell you what happened after that, but I don't know. Of one thing I am certain, though: here was a prime example of a person who was unable to get away completely from ideas and ideals and practices that had been a vital part of his life.

Dr. William James, a noted psychologist of a few

decades ago, said, in speaking of the effect of evil thinking and evil behavior, "God may forgive, but one's nervous system never forgets if it [evil] is apt to be allowed to enter and find lodgment."

Is it a filthy story to which we are going to listen and give our approval today? Is it a sensational, overdrawn, perhaps malicious paper, magazine, or speech to which we will give assent? Is it a lie, a fraud, some crooked deal in which we are planning to participate, some vulgar or unkind habit that we are allowing to creep slowly upon us? As a result of this day's experience we can expect only one thing: a cheapening of our values, which may be forgiven by a loving Father and which may never be displayed publicly as were the habits of the drunken circus barker, but which will weaken our judgment and our struggles from this day until the end of life.

> The Moving Finger writes; and, having writ,
> Moves on: nor all thy Piety nor Wit
> Shall lure it back to cancel half a Line,
> Nor all thy Tears wash out a Word of it.
> —Edward Fitzgerald

Hence it becomes comparatively easy for us to determine pretty definitely today what our personalities will look like tomorrow. There is nothing mysterious about the process of development, for the body can be no more than the food that goes into it, and not even that much without proper exercise. Thus, the mind, the personality, and the character of any one of us can be no greater than the thoughts upon which they feed, and indeed not even that without the proper expression.

If you want to be a man or woman of cheap, illiterate, uncouth personality, with low ideals and little power of self-control, shuffling along through life as a slave to passion and injurious habits, all you have to do is feed your mind every day on cheap, trashy, insipid, vicious, vulgar thoughts and allow them to find expression in habit, and you will have little trouble in accomplishing your goal. On the other hand, if you want to be a man or a woman with a strong mind and beautiful personality, happy in your knowledge of self-achievement and in the respect of your fellowmen, you need only to feed your mind on the more wholesome thoughts of life and allow those thoughts to find expression in daily habit. You will then be certain to attain this goal.

We are told that the poet Schiller cried out during the latter days of his life and, indeed, almost in his very last breath: "Give me a great thought. Give me a great thought!" Now I am asking you, as you read this chapter, to say with me—and to pay the price of saying—"Give us great thoughts—wholesome, clean, uplifting thoughts and habits." For as truly as the sun rises and sets, and the determination to build those thoughts comes and goes with the seasons, whatsoever we sow in our minds (and this is no pet theology or a thunderbolt from the hand of God, but a principle upon which we may always depend)–whatsoever we sow in our minds today, we will reap in our souls tomorrow. We make our own choice, we sow our own seed, we harvest our own crop, and it is ours to decide whether it shall be good or bad.

"Thou shalt not bear false witness . . ."

—Exodus 20:16

13

Adjusting Our Glasses

I've been told that President Woodrow Wilson had a pretty long nose and that he often wore his glasses near the end of his nose. Upon being asked for the reason of this practice he jokingly replied, "I wear my glasses near the end of my nose so that I can always see what I'm talking about."

If more people followed some such practice, figuratively speaking, there would probably be much less trouble in the world today. Too many of us "spout off at the mouth" without seeing clearly what we are talking about.

"Why, Brother Dunn, I tell you it's just awful," said a student to me one day, as he expressed his disgust at something that was going on at the institute of religion. "Why, I never heard anything like it before. If something isn't done immediately to stop the whole affair that—that—that—," and away he went to another person and then another, to spread the news, until most of the institute student body was finally aroused to a pitch of frenzy. At last, after we had a few moments to investigate, we discovered that the report was only about one-fifth true. No real sin had been committed by those accused, and the peddler of the false report had to admit that he had not seen the thing in the proper light. In other words, he had not worn his glasses close enough to his mouth.

A certain General Authority picked up a newspaper not long ago and, seeing an article that concerned his own statements, began to read only to find that a statement was accredited to him that was totally out of context and that in a sense he had never made. By this time the falsehood had no doubt gone to every corner of the state, for the newspaper had quite a large following; and the wrongly accused brother will pay the penalty in the esteem of his brothers and sisters not because a writer had meant to be dishonest, but because he had not worn his glasses close enough to his talking machine. He had scattered poisonous words without taking the trouble to know what he was talking or writing about.

"Oh, I'm so sorry! So sorry!" is a common expression of many people who seem to take this word as an antidote for all the poison one can spill. How much better it would be to feel sorry enough for the last mistake that we would promise never to let an accusation of any kind pass our lips until we have investigated enough to see for a certainty what we are talking about.

I'm always interested in watching the bank teller to see how he carefully examines every check and note and how cautiously he hands out, counting and sometimes recounting, every bill that is received. When you stop to think about it, we are all bankers, often holding within ourselves the fortunes of a great many people. Do we really examine the life reports that come to us as carefully as the bank teller examines the lifeless checks that come into his hands? If bankers accepted at face value as many faulty signatures and counterfeit bills as we take into our lives in life reports, they'd go broke overnight. And if when we hand out reports we were as careful to count every word as the bank teller is to count every dollar and every cent, I have a feeling that we would not give away so easily another's fortune, another's reputation that we hold within our power. Gossip can be a vicious thing; it has ruined countless reputations, mostly through untruths.

The Savior warned against this pernicious evil: "Thou shalt not bear false witness." Old Testament prophets also warned against this practice.

It all goes back to the old problem of not seeing what we are talking about before we begin to talk. I don't believe that very many, if any, of the people who claim the name of Christ would maliciously ruin another person's good name. But the results are just the same whether we act criminally or carelessly, whether we speak brutally or blindly. It may be that some of us need a change of heart. I imagine that at least the majority, if not all, of us need an occasional readjustment of our mental glasses, bringing them down so close to our lips that no harsh words will ever escape without first being properly counted and properly appraised.

"There are a thousand hacking at the branches of evil to one who is striking at the root."

—Thoreau

14

Courtesy on the Road

A speaker once told of a man who started to get into his car and, on the way, unintentionally brushed against the arm of a passing woman. "Sorry," he said sincerely. "Most clumsy of me."

"Not at all," replied the woman with a smile, as she moved on toward her own car.

Soon both of them were in their separate cars going down the road when, at a corner, one crashed into the other. No real damage was done to either car, but as the two individuals stepped out to see what had happened, they became quite upset, the woman saying loudly to the man, "Why don't you watch the signals?"

And he responded with, "What's the matter with your signals, lady? You women drivers give me a pain in the neck!"

The simple act of stepping off the curb and into a car had turned both of these individuals into semi-barbarians and changed them from agreeable social creatures into bad-mannered, quarrelsome bores.

The story amused me at first, but the more I thought about it, and especially when I endeavored to relate it to the traffic problems this country is now faced with, there kept coming back to my mind those words of the great philosopher Thoreau: "There are a thousand hacking at the branches of evil to one who is striking at the root."

Are you aware that we have an annual economic loss, due to automobile accidents, of several billion dollars a year, and hundreds of thousands of personal injuries, to say nothing of the thousands of fatalities that occur every year in the United States alone?

As you can see, this presents a real menace to the life and happiness of our people. How are we going to meet the difficulty except by hacking at the branches—finding a few who disobey the laws and putting others in jail—when all of us know that the only way to solve the problem is for every one of us as individuals, together with all other folks who really want to be good citizens, to strike from our hearts the root of discourtesy?

I call it discourtesy because to me that's what it appears to be. Perhaps it is just not thinking, or the occasional rebel who thinks the highway is made personally for him. Other vehicles, such as motorcycles, often provide our roads with a great menace. Not long ago I was following several motorcyclists down a mountain road, and they deliberately got into formation so that no one on the highway could pass. I noticed several drivers behind me were tempted to "run them down," and had the highway not opened into a valley, I'm sure some great catastrophe could easily have occurred.

We punish people for carrying concealed weapons, and yet the majority of our people carry about with them, when they travel on the road, a spirit of discourtesy that is largely responsible for the loss of many billions of dollars and thousands of lives in a single year.

This situation has gone beyond the joking point, and I challenge all of us, as true-hearted citizens, to begin now, this very day, to carry into our cars the same courteous spirit that we display in practically every other relationship in life. It is a call to citizenship to every decent man and woman who drives. It is a simple display of our concern for the life, freedom, and happiness of our people. It is really the gospel in action.

"Let not your heart be troubled: ye believe in God, believe also in me. . . . whatsoever ye shall ask in my name, that will I do."

—John 14:1, 13

15

Making the Sick Call

I'd like to come into the room of the shut-in and, if I may, chat with you for a few moments. It must be pretty tough to be laid up on a day like this—to see the rest of us walking around, hale and hardy, and to know that you must remain on your back. It is easy for those of us who are up to tell you who are down how to smile in the midst of adversity, and so much more difficult for us to say the same thing if we were in your place and you in ours. I've often noticed that the people who have never been in trouble generally make the most beautiful and flowery statements about how to behave when trouble comes.

The man who is worthwhile is the man who can smile when everything goes completely wrong. Yes, but some very worthwhile people often find themselves in positions in which smiling is difficult, if not a hypocritical practice. It is natural for babies to cry when struck by pain. It is natural for animals to bellow and scream when injured or frightened, and natural for the bravest and strongest of good men and women to lose their poise at times. You may recall that even our Savior on two occasions, one when facing and later in the ordeal of physical suffering, gave voice to his anguish of heart.

Perhaps it would help you a little, therefore, those of you who are sick or afflicted, to realize that your worry is not an awful sin nor is it necessarily a sign of weakness. Being human, you have a right occasionally to be discouraged, and even at times to give way to your despair. It would be unfortunate, however, for you not to see the evidences of hope that are round about you.

For instance, look at your hands. The skin does not appear to be moving, but we know that every square inch of our body is made up of myriads of molecules that are in constant motion. Your heart, as I have learned in recent months, is pumping away all the time; the lungs are active; and, in fact, practically every part of your body is doing its best to bring you back to health. Mother Nature is a strict parent and will accept no alibis, but she is also wonderfully kind. And really, isn't it surprising what she can do for the person who through patience and proper care will only give her a chance! The thing to remember is that she is busy on the job at this very moment and that at every minute of every day and night she is actively engaged in the process of trying to bring you back to health.

Perhaps it would help you also to realize that even as you lie flat on your back in bed, you can do much to aid Mother Nature in this task. Jesus taught this fact. His disciples believed it, and reputable physicians place stress upon it. I am speaking about the powerful influence of the mind upon the body. For instance, why do you blush? Because of some thought. Why does your face turn white? Because of fear. What happens when you think of some ordeal through which you must pass (even if it is only that of making your first talk or singing your first song in public)? Your lips become dry; your knees literally shake; and your nerves are definitely affected by thoughts. And you also have the power to control your thoughts.

If for some reason you may never regain perfect health, remember that opportunities of service and satisfaction still await you. A medium-sized fellow crippled in one leg has become the head of one of the finest and largest car dealerships in the Salt Lake City area, is a great athlete on the tennis court, and has many other marvelous accomplishments. Another example: a patient who some time ago was in a hospital with a terrible case of sinus trouble and who is now on his feet, still seriously handicapped with his physical difficulty, but one of the most charitable and efficient surgeons in Los Angeles. A third example: a woman who for many years has been a hopeless cripple, confined to a wheelchair, and always in pain—the result of a very serious illness—yet who has adjusted to her fate so beautifully that she attends to her church service, keeps house, and with the sweetest of all dispositions I have ever seen is today an inspiration to scores of other people.

And do not forget, through it all, the words of the Master Teacher: "Let not your heart be troubled: ye believe in God, believe also in me. . . . whatsoever ye shall ask in my name, that will I do, that the Father may be glorified in the Son." (John 14:1, 13.)

The Lord loveth a cheerful giver, and one of the best things to give is a cheerful acceptance of what others give to you.

A Cheerful Receiver

I have a new text to share in this chapter, not taken from the scriptures, but from the unwritten Book of Life. In the scriptures we are told that the Lord loveth a cheerful giver. In the Book of Life we are told that the Lord and humanity loveth a cheerful receiver.

We have heard much about the value of giving, having had placed before us so often the admonition: "It is more blessed to give than to receive." I imagine most of us would agree that many people are unhappy today because they have not learned to give. But I am also convinced that there are hosts of people who have made themselves and others miserable because they have not learned how to accept the kindness of others in a cheerful way.

Some are like this because they are socially blind and unable to see anything about them but baseness and selfishness. "There is no kindness for which to be grateful," they say, but I have not found this to be so. Last summer, I experienced an unexpected illness. During my life I have enjoyed excellent health and have never known many days in bed. Then, the seeming tragedy. During the many weeks and months of recuperation, day in day out, almost hourly, came the human kindnesses from around the world, the little thoughts, the prayers, the flowers, the cards, the letters, the concern of others. This was something I had never experienced before, for I had always been in the kind of work where I was trying to give rather than to receive.

What a great blessing of the gospel was learned: to be able to accept cheerfully the gracious offers and little helps in our behalf, knowing that they came from the hearts of wonderful Christians and neighbors. Beautiful letters of appreciation, poems, and interesting articles have come from people whose names I have never heard, all because they wanted to share their feelings of concern and love and affection. They have extended these courtesies because the heart of humanity in the main, when it is not worried or persecuted or in pain, would rather be kind than unkind.

The complexities of life today have made us extraordinarily cautious and have so guarded the spirit of kindness that it does not always show on the surface. But if it sees a chance to safely come out in the open, it will be agreeably received. One does not have to look long or far to find himself surrounded on every side by evidences of brotherly appreciation.

One of the reasons I say that some people can never know the blessing of another's kindness is that they see in every kind act a trick that another is trying to play, or some benefit or gain, or perhaps an extra obligation that the kind acts of another places upon him.

I'm thinking of one such person right now: morally good, anxious to help others, but nearly the most lonesome, common, woebegone mortal that I know, a man who is actually worrying his life away because he is too blind or too stubborn (and sometimes, I think, too selfish) to acknowledge the kindnesses that others show toward him. He said recently after some friends had bestowed a kindness upon him, "The only reason they do this is to make me think they're good." I can hear him saying after someone has paid him a compliment, "The old hypocrite! He doesn't mean a word of it. Just trying to get on the good side of me—or if not that, at least to make me feel better by a lot of flattery."

Poor fellow! And there are many suspicious souls like him who are missing much of the thrill of life because they are unwilling to take a chance on the natural kindness of human nature. It is far better to be grateful for the good that others think they find in us. The Lord loveth a cheerful giver, and one of the best things to give is a cheerful acceptance of what others give to you.

"He that is without sin among you, let him first cast a stone. . . ."

—John 8:7

17

Engines and People

A few summers ago I traveled through Arizona and into California with my family, and we were enjoying every minute of the trip. It was one of those rare chances for us to be together without interruption. It was a pretty warm day, and I suddenly became conscious of the fact that our car was losing all of its power. For a few moments it coasted and then at a slight rise in the road it stopped dead still. I looked around and discovered that I had plenty of gas, the radiator was full of water, the fan belt was in place, and the oil level was at least where it ought to have been, so I knew that the trouble was not in the overheated engine.

A friendly traveler took me to a phone several miles up the road where I called a garage; in a while a mechanic arrived where we were parked beside the road. Almost immediately sensing the difficulties, he stuck the sharp end of a pen through a tiny hole at the top of the carburetor, and the car was ready to go again. He had found a tiny speck of dirt so small that it could hardly be seen by the naked eye, yet it had been able to stop the progress of a whole family for about two hours, cause one of us to walk a considerable distance, and change the plans for the entire party that night and for the rest of the trip.

Since that experience I've been thinking that it's not only the cars and carefree travelers, but the work of whole institutions and the plans of communities and nations, that are sometimes held up by tiny specks of dirt that thoughtless people put in the way. Reports and gossip columnists in newspapers, magazines, and other media are often guilty of this. For some reason or another, they seem to thrive on discovering and magnifying the dirt in other people's lives. What better news, we are led to believe, than that some talented artist, civic leader, or national public figure has made a mistake. And so, upon the discovery of such, these reporters give a shout of triumph and, with the dirtiest black ink, spread the news, with the result being that the influence of a good life is held up and sometimes practically destroyed. And the worst of it is that once the dirt has been brought to life and magnified, no living public mechanic can completely destroy it.

Reporters and gossip columnists are not the only collectors of dirt. It seems to me that in every college group and every club and every community to which I have belonged there have been a few persons who have felt it their duty to ferret out and advertise all the mistakes that their leaders have ever made. "Once a sinner, always a sinner!" we are told—not because the masses of people would have it so (most folks are probably willing to help the underdog), but the task of forgetting and letting a person repent is made extremely difficult because of the scavengers who will not let the sin be forgotten.

A stranger in a community makes good. Arriving as a young man in a town on the West Coast, he proves his worth by honest labor and helpful cooperation. He wins a place of confidence in the hearts of the people. He marries a daughter of one of the best families and begins rearing a happy family. Then along comes an acquaintance of ten years past who begins to whisper: "Have you not heard?

Did no one ever tell you of his previous experiences?" And with the aid of a few light-minded souls, and through a vicious whispering campaign, he is able after a week or two not only to ruin the influence of a good man, but also to break the hopes and drag down the reputations of a loyal wife and children.

We have seen this so prominently in the national image of our country in recent months. Have we no sense of justice in our hearts? Would you and I be willing, before criticizing the mistakes of others, to stand before our club or church or school or community and disclose all of the mistakes of which we have been guilty in the past?

I recall that on one occasion some critical folks brought a woman to Jesus condemning her for past mistakes. The Master said calmly, "He that is without sin among you, let him first cast a stone at her"—and when they heard it, "they went out one by one, beginning at the eldest, even unto the last." Then Jesus said calmly and encouragingly to the woman: "Neither do I condemn thee: go, and sin no more." (See John 8:7-11.)

Dust and dirt, the mistakes of a former day! Oh yes, we all have them, and it doesn't take any great intelligence to find them. Almost any gossiper who happens to know the facts and who brings them to the light and magnifies them a little could cause us no end of inconvenience.

So I hope that I shall not have to walk several miles over a hot highway for the purpose of getting a tiny speck of dirt out of my car's engine. I am glad for one such experience if it will continue to remind me of the damage that I can do by throwing dirt into the mental and moral machinery of my fellowmen and my country.

*"Take what God gives, oh heart,
and build your heart of happiness
today."*

—B.Y. Williams

18

Comparative Values

Have you ever gotten up on the wrong side of the bed? I guess we've all had such occasions in our lives, some mornings being better than others. I remember one such experience that occurred some time ago.

About ten o'clock one evening I received word from a faculty member of a group that I was coordinating in Southern California that he would be unable to teach his class on a distant campus that next day. He wondered if I would mind substituting for him, because it was an extreme emergency. After assuring him that I would fill in, I checked the assignment and what was expected of me. Then I retired and went right to sleep.

I was enjoying my rest for the first hour or so when, at about two o'clock, I was awakened by one of my daughters, who insisted that she must have a drink—she simply could not get along without it until morning. So, after a hard struggle, I pulled myself together, got her a drink of water, and went back to bed only to be awakened an hour later by another daughter who had accidently pushed her doll out of bed and who felt that it would be quite impossible to go to sleep until the doll was retrieved.

After another effort to pull myself from between warm covers, pick up the doll, and retire once more with the hope that the few remaining hours would be of peace and rest, I was brought slowly back to consciousness by the last member of the tribe who had just had a beautiful dream and could she tell it to me before she forgot? Added to all of this, when I finally came to my senses, were thoughts of certain bills that must be paid and a before-the-end-of-the-year general depression that somehow could not be moved.

And then it happened—the little thing that changed the gloom of the night into the brightness of a beautiful day and changed my whole attitude for several days that followed.

As I was leaving for my teaching assignment, one of the little daughters who had been guilty of keeping me awake part of the night pulled on my coat, and, with help, climbed to my shoulders, gave a yank on my ear and nose, and said, "Daddy, you're sure a good sport."

A good sport, huh? I tried to smile away the frown that had settled throughout my whole system.

"Yep! You're the best dad in all the world," she said. Then, slapping a kiss on my mouth, she slid to the floor and ran away. And I had worried about hard times—with the confidence and the love of a little daughter that I would not trade for all the comforts and the wealth that life could provide!

I hope you will pardon me for sharing one of my own experiences. I do it merely to urge those of us who get up with a bad taste in our mouths, who fuss about every little difficulty and who worry because we cannot have all the material things that we would like to have, to stop for a moment and count our many blessings, naming them one by one: children whose love and companionship cannot be measured in dollars and cents, a loyal wife or husband for whom we would gladly give our life, if necessary; friends whose loyalty brings comfort and satisfactions that wealth could never bring. I remember during a recent illness receiving this beautiful poem by B. Y. Williams:

Take what God gives, oh heart of mine, and build your house of happiness.
Perchance some have been given more, but many have been given less.
The treasure lying at your feet whose value you but think to guess
Another builder looking on would barter Heaven to possess.

Trust not tomorrow, tomorrow's dawns to bring,
The dreams of joy—dreamed of for which you wait;
You have enough of pleasant things to house your soul in goodly state.
Tomorrow, time's relentless stream may bear what you have now away.
Take what God gives, oh heart, and build your heart of happiness today!

"Down in their hearts, wise men know this truth: the only way to help yourself is to help others."

—Elbert Hubbard

19

A Salute to Doctors

My wife's father shared this story with us many years ago. He said that in a little southern Illinois town the rain had been falling in great sheets for about two days and nights, much resembling a continuous cloudburst, and as a result the mud was so deep in the roads and the bridges so wobbly—those bridges that had not yet been washed away—that it was hardly safe to travel even in the light of day.

Night came, and with the stroke of midnight came the telephone bell, calling to some danger or trouble along the way. "Yes—this is the doctor. You say it happened this evening and that you are now in great pain? I'm awfully sorry, but I don't see how it would be possible to come tonight. Such a trip would be at the risk of my own life. What's that? Oh, buck up, old man, of course it hurts. Endure it as best you can until morning, and I will then move heaven and earth to reach you." But as the doctor caught the moan of despair across the line, he continued, "All right, my friend, I'll be there as fast as I can make it."

After quickly slipping into his clothes, he ran to the barn, hitched his trusty team of horses to the old one-seated buggy, and drove out into the mud—mile after mile, with the wheels sinking almost hub deep in some places. Torrents of rain poured down from dark clouds above, lightning flashed and thunder pounded on every side, as the lone country doctor gambled his own life for the sake of his fellowman.

Suddenly, without a moment's warning, the wheels slipped and the team of horses plunged headlong into the water of a swiftly moving stream. There was no time to think. The young doctor, pulling himself from the buggy, swam quickly to the heads of his horses, unfastened enough of the harness to loosen them from the buggy, and swam with them safely to the other shore. Then, after a look back at the little buggy—most of which was covered with water and within which, at the bottom of the stream, were his robes and medicine case—he gave a little sigh, jumped to the back of one of his horses, and, leading the other behind him with a strap, continued his perilous journey of mercy.

That is all of the story I remember hearing. Did the young doctor reach the home in time to save the life, or did he reach it at all that night? I cannot tell. But I know that he stands as one among thousands in his profession who count no danger too great and no chance too perilous if it is necessary to the saving of a human life. I salute them all as benefactors of the human race. After spending from eight to as many as twelve years in college, several years in internships and residencies, and generally living on little for the first few years of their practice, they finally gain a place of prominence and then spend much of their time in the service of others, often risking their own lives and the lives of their families in the process. They face constant demands to learn new ideas and new techniques and new methods, each of which, as it is applied, brings new life to many of their patients. Think what has been accomplished medically in the past decade compared with previous generations.

There is not a single hour of the day or night that a

conscientious doctor can really call his own. He is often misunderstood, seldom completely obeyed, and then blamed if the patient fails to recover. He carries about with him all the time, waking and sleeping, the responsibility of helping his fellowman, with the relentless realization that a single wrong act on his part or a word of incorrect advice may bring death instead of life.

"Of course, that's only part of his job," you say, but I think that if all of us would resolve to be in our own tasks as thoughtful of the good of our fellowmen as are the majority of doctors, this would be a better world in which to live. Thank God for these great men of mercy, and a salute to them is certainly in order!

A simple, old-fashioned dictum:
Be fair.

20

Advice for Seniors

Often I have the opportunity to stand before high school and college graduating classes and try to fulfill the challenge of giving counsel and advice to those who are about to leave the halls of learning. I remember standing before one graduating class with the thought on my mind to say, "Be honest." But that is not enough. One may be honest and vulgar, or honest and cruel. I thought of saying, "Be kind and loving toward all whom you meet." But how many of us can understand the full meaning of those words?

At last, after traveling about among many words and phrases, I have come back to the simple, old-fashioned dictum: "Be fair." Be as fair as President Herbert Hoover, who, when learning of his defeat, said, "I have lost, but I shall be as loyal to those who have defeated me as I would have wished them to be to me if I had won." Be as fair with truth as the college professor who, after spending years in writing a book on science and discovering one little fact that disproved his theory, withdrew his book and began the task of rewriting it. Be as fair as the Master, who, although misunderstood and mistreated by those whom he attempted to help, continued to love them and to help them, and finally to die for them, because, he said, "They know not what they do."

Now, I know that it is exceedingly difficult to be so fair, but I am convinced that it is possible, if we will remember and practice the following suggestions faithfully.

Before attempting to form any judgment or to say or do anything that may cause sorrow or misunderstanding, we should be sure we have all the facts in hand. I venture to say that the majority of tragedies involving human relations might easily be averted if folks only knew all the facts.

To illustrate, two business people had a misunderstanding, and the feeling grew into hatred, their business relations were stopped, and they would no longer speak to each other. After several months, the difficulty was discovered. One man had said something about the other that was perfectly harmless, and the words were quoted by a third party. The words were accurate, but it was the difference in the tone of voice that changed a harmless statement into one of poison.

But it is not enough just to know the facts. One day while I was riding with some friends along a highway, we had quite a discussion about the beauty of the surrounding environment.

"How beautiful," said one of my friends.

"I can't see anything beautiful about it," another said. "It is so dull and unsightly."

"Why," said my friend, "you're certainly mistaken. It's a most attractive and inspiring scene."

"I can't see it that way," the other said. Then he raised his hand to his face to wipe away some perspiration, and he discovered that he was wearing a pair of very dark colored sunglasses. When he took them off, he realized that he had been wrong; the scene was truly pretty, bright, and beautiful. The glasses had played the trick.

And so it is that dark emotions, such as anger, suspicion, fear, and self-pride, may come between our minds and our normal situations, making fools of our judgment and causing us, with all the facts directly in front of us, to arrive at conclusions that are entirely unfair to the situation at hand.

So I say to seniors everywhere, members of any graduating class, if you can keep your heads when the world is becoming excited about every upheaval; if you can be patient when the mobs are crying for persecution and vengeance; if, in a word, you can be fair, noting before every conclusion you make or every harmful deed you might do all of the available facts and then, without malice or anger or fear but in the spirit of good sportsmanship, give credit where credit is due, you will help to lay the foundation stones of a true democracy. And as a consequence, you will also prove a reason for an educational system that, with all its mistakes, is still fundamentally gospel-centered at heart.

"He approaches nearest to the Gods who knows how to be silent, even though he is in the right."

—Anonymous

21

Cracked

Did you ever have an experience like this one that happened to me some years ago? It was late at night and we were taking some of our family home after having been out to dinner. We'd traveled several miles—our trusty car running as smoothly as one could wish—when, as we started up a steep hill, and without any warning, the engine began to knock. The steering wheel shook in my hand and the car began to shake all over as though it had a nervous chill. We managed to get to the top of the hill, deposit our passengers at their homes, coast back down the hill, and, with much shaking and sputtering, finally reached our home in safety.

The next morning, with two long trips scheduled for the day, I drove the car into a nearby station and watched as the mechanic lifted the hood and applied the side of a screwdriver to the engine in an effort to locate the trouble. Finally, stopping at one point, he unfastened a wire, removed a sparkplug, and, after examining it carefully, looked up and said, "It's cracked."

"You mean the sparkplug is cracked?"

"Yes," he said, "and that is the cause of all your

difficulty." A single crack in a little sparkplug could change the behavior of an entire car? "Well, if you don't believe it, I'll show you." Taking out a new sparkplug, he screwed it in, fastened the wire, put down the hood, and said, "Now go out and see for yourself whether I've told you the truth."

Well, I discovered immediately that he knew his business. And as I drove home enjoying the smooth, even tone of a properly running engine, noting the difference between its present condition and that of the old lumber-wagon that I had driven into the station a few moments before, I began to think about certain people whom I had known.

One was a very knowledgeable teacher in a community where I used to live who talked as smoothly and as fluently as anyone I have ever heard, as long as he discoursed on subjects he was skilled in; but as soon as he began to talk about topics with which he was not acquainted, he suddenly lost all of his logic and his usual smoothness was gone. He sputtered and shook and became as different from his other self as my shaky car was different from the smooth-running automobile. You see, in a very real sense, he had a cracked sparkplug that affected his whole being.

What did this man believe about the particular subjects in which he had no training? I don't even remember, but that is not the point; everyone has a right to his own convictions about everything if he really tries to know the truth, and no real gentleman will show disrespect when those opinions are freely expressed. But no man has a right, because of the effect that it has upon himself and his family, to become so enamored with his pet opinions that he loses all sense of mental emotional proportion. That was the trouble with this teacher: reasonable, agreeable, intelligent enough part of the time, but a shaky, disagreeable old crab when his cracked sparkplug came into play.

Another example is the college professor who, because he has specific training in one or two particular fields, takes license to pass himself off as a specialist in all fields. I think this is one of the greatest dangers facing our young people. Just because a man has a doctorate in a particular discipline, this does not qualify him for all disciplines.

I thought about another person, a most delightful personality—highly educated, thoroughly unselfish—who will do anything to help a person in trouble. However, he is so obsessed with a certain political view that he can hardly talk to anyone for a few minutes without feeling that he must convert the other person to his own point of view. And when he gets started—well, it's just like that old car with a bad sparkplug. He fuses and sputters and becomes one of the most cantankerous individuals you ever saw. You know, it's really too bad, because while this person, who has such fine training and natural ability, could be a leader for good in his community, it has come to the point that people can hardly speak of him without smiling, and they rather hesitate to invite him into a crowd.

You know such a person, don't you? Oh, I'm sure you don't know the name of the particular person I have in mind, but there is one in your life. Have you ever asked yourself, What could be done to repair these troublesome, cracked sparkplugs that turn otherwise smooth-running people into sputtering social nuisances? Would you suggest that these people keep on using their favorite sparkplugs and merely try to repair them a little so that they will not shake so illogically and emotionally when put into play? That was what I thought about as I watched the mechanic fix my car. Since my sparkplug was only cracked, I asked myself if it would not be wise to have it patched up a little and try to use it some more. Why spend a couple of dollars for a new plug when you could repair an old one? But on second thought I realized that even if this could be done, it would take so much time and trouble that maybe the old plug could not be depended upon—that it would be better to throw it away and put a new one in its place.

I'm not so sure but that this might not be the best procedure for the one who insists on being socially or politically cracked and who really needs a new plug. Most of these folks have been using the old sparkplug so long that they would find it practically impossible to give it the proper repair. Perhaps the best thing for them to do would be to take the old plug out and to insert in its place the open mind. One old sage said some years ago that the so-called open mind occasionally ought to be closed for repairs.

I think one of the great virtues that we can develop is to restrain the tongue; as one has said, "He approaches nearest to the Gods who knows how to be silent, even though he is in the right."

". . . ye shall know the truth, and the truth shall make you free."

—John 8:32

22

What Is Freedom?

Many years ago while I was serving in the infantry during World War II, it was my privilege as an American soldier to be engaged in a number of battles. During one of those campaigns on an island in the Pacific, my particular platoon drew the assignment to secure a military objective several miles into the jungle. On our reconnaissance, lo and behold, we came upon an enemy concentration camp. Incarcerated in this camp were some 2,500 to 3,000 natives. The enemy had abandoned the camp several minutes before, and I was honored to be one of the few soldiers to break down the barriers and bring freedom to this anxious group.

Words cannot describe the filth and misery that these people had experienced during their three years of imprisonment. Many children had been born under this extreme condition, where sickness and malnutrition were rampant. As we were hastily preparing to evacuate these unfortunate people to the beach area, I was standing inside of the camp and was startled to feel a thump on my boot. Looking down in the mud, I found the form of a man perhaps in his sixties who was barely recognizable as being alive. Upon examining him closer, I found that he was an American minister who had been trapped in the jungle and eventually taken prisoner by the enemy. Even though he was approximately six feet tall, he weighed less than 100 pounds, and huge sores covered his body. As he struggled to gain some strength, his first request of me was, "Soldier, do you have an American flag?" I told him I did not have one on me, but I thought I could secure one. After sending word to one of our jeep drivers to see if he could find one, we prepared a stretcher and tried to bring the man as much physical comfort as possible under those conditions. We cleaned the mud from his face, gave him a drink of water, and administered minor first aid. When the flag was brought to us, I handed it to him. With tears in his eyes, he placed it over his bosom, and said, "Thank God you have come!" In a very real sense I, an eighteen-year-old soldier, saw in the face of a man who had experienced terrible tragedy the true meaning of physical freedom.

Freedom has many definitions. Let me share a few from some great philosophers. It was Einstein who said, "I do not believe in taking a philosophic meaning of the term the freedom of man. Every man acts not only as a result of outside influences, but also because of an inner need." Voltaire gave us this definition: "I told you that man's freedom consists of his power to act, and out of the miraculous power to want, to desire." Silone said, "The man who thinks with his head is a free man. The man who fights for what he believes is right is a free man. Freedom is not begged from others; freedom must be taken." Spinozo said, "Men are mistaken in believing that they are free, and this opinion is that they are conscious of their actions, but yet they are unaware of the causes by which they are determined; therefore, their idea of freedom is that they are not aware of the causes of their actions." Bergson has said, "Freedom is a reality, and among all existing truths, there are none which are clearer." Descartes said, "Our freedom to choose does not need to be proven for the mere reason that we have experienced it." R. P. Lacordaire made this observation: "Do not ask why man is free; he is free because he chooses what he will love." Tagore said, "How easy it is to crush, in the name of the exterior freedom, the internal freedom of man."

So what is freedom? The Savior has said, ". . . ye shall know the truth, and the truth shall make you free." (John 8:32.) Is not ignorance, in reality, an obstacle to our freedom? Is it not ignorance that causes us to suffer, to lose our way, to be deceived? Freedom permits us to use laws; therefore, we must first know them. Is knowledge an end in itself? Most certainly not! We still must act, know who we are or what we can hope for and attain, and how we can achieve it.

Someone has said that "our emotions hinder our search. They take possession of us, suggesting to us that it is normal to follow our physical impulses. If they are natural, let's give in to them." Where would such a way of thinking lead us? If freedom were the possibility to follow our desires, we would certainly be free; however, the experience of mankind demonstrates the contrary. We bring alienation upon ourselves.

How many have given up their freedom for the desires of their bodies or their minds? There is no longer a question of freedom for the dope addict, enslaved to his drugs. No, that is not freedom. Freedom is in the very depths of each one of us. It is, as Tagore said, "the internal freedom of man." It is the decision we can make to progress in righteousness.

The Church teaches us that we are sons and daughters of God. Here is a lofty ideal that gives our freedom its true meaning. No more hindrance, ignorance, or passion; by surmounting obstacles we become more free, and in choosing the right, we increase our freedom. Each decision made, each action taken will make us, according to its nature, either more liberated or more captive. In reality, the truth shall make us free.

"Put on the whole armour of God . . ."

—Ephesians 6:11

23

A Militant People

Is it ever proper for a person to become angry? I believe that it is. Surely the Creator would not have given us a temper if he had not expected us to use it for some good purpose.

When a group of politicians purposely hold up the passing of laws that are needed for the good of the weaker members of society; when some lawyers are allowed to misrepresent a case in court and, for the sake of winning a point, send honest men to jail, or after much trickery clear those whom they know to be deserving of imprisonment; when a few vulgar-minded movie producers are permitted to ruin the ideals of our children and young people and at the same time put into dispute the reputation of other actors and producers who are endeavoring to provide a wholesome form of entertainment—I say, whenever people who enjoy the benefits of this country deliberately plan, for the sake of their own material gain, to bring anything but justice and fair play to any group of people, it is time for self-respecting citizens to become angry. I did not say lose control of their tempers, but to become angry and resolve not to rest until they have helped to change these conditions.

It is not necessary to hate another person; however, it is necessary to hate with intense hatred any practice that tends to deprive one individual or any group of deserving individuals of the opportunities of abundant life. Jesus Christ drove the dishonest money changers from the temple. The scriptures don't say that he asked them to retire; it says that he cast them out "and overthrew the tables of the moneychangers, and the seats of them that sold the doves" (Matthew 21:12), not because of the business in which they were engaged, but because of the crooked way in which they used their power to defraud those who came for help.

I am convinced that one of the main reasons why respectable citizens have not been more successful in cleaning up the nation is because they have not allowed themselves to become sufficiently disturbed about the injustices and vulgarities and snares that bad people have thrown about them. The principle of loving the enemies of society and even praying for those who mistreat defenseless people is in no way violated by an active war upon the evil deeds that these people perform. And while it is fine to have faith in God, one must not expect him to clear up social conditions while we sit back in our comfortable chairs and take our ease.

I notice that gangsters don't come around in half-apologetic fashion and say, "Now, if it suits your convenience, we should like to have you hand over a little of your coin." The traitors who make a laughingstock of our Constitution, who for the sake of selfish gain exploit womanhood and childhood, the ruffians who trample roughshod over the sacred things of life, are not going to be controlled by simply praying for a better world. If the Church and other interested institutions in society are to fulfill their obligation of bringing the kingdom of heaven to earth, we must realize and recognize that to be a true Latter-day Saint means to engage in a constant warfare—not against people or nations, but against sin—a battle that has as its motive the putting down of graft and injustice and oppression, whether they are to be found in business, politics, education, or even in religion itself.

"Kill the sin, and save the sinner" is a motto that, if adopted and followed courageously and consistently by every church and synagogue of this nation, would not only greatly increase the prestige of organized religion, but also do much to clear our streets and our business houses and our government and our homes of crime, making this a safe place in which to rear our children and enjoy the fellowship of honest men and women.

The apostle Paul had the idea when he said: "Put on the whole armour of God [not of a militaristic organization], for we wrestle not against flesh and blood, but against principalities, against powers, against the rulers of the darkness of this world, against spiritual wickedness in high places." (Ephesians 6:11-12.) The need for divine courage and righteous indignation is as great today as in the time in which Paul first gave this stirring challenge of a war against sin and on behalf of both the righteous and the sinful peoples of a darkened world.

Try consciously to keep your feelings in tune with the feelings of those about you.

24

Tender Courtesies

Do you want to know what I consider a real day's work? Taking care of three lively youngsters for two hours when their mother is away from home, or spending twenty minutes with the same youngsters in a grocery store: trying to fill a basket with groceries while one youngster opens a cookie box, another tries to pick up and then drops a bottle of pickles, and the third, lost somewhere on the other side of the store, startles the entire community with her frightened, "Oh, Daddy—Daddy—Daddy!"

Try standing calm and unperturbed while the cashier adds up the bill and three sleight-of-hand performers wonder if this piece of candy or gum placed conveniently near the check-out counter wouldn't be better than that one, or isn't that package of goodies larger than the one we didn't aim to buy anyway.

Then if you want another day's work, take the children home to find that the mother has been detained; fill up their hungry stomachs for them, put three sets of pajamas on the most wriggly pieces of humanity you ever saw, send them off to bed, and behold! the calm that surpasses all understanding!

I tell you, men—and I believe my day is as long and nerve-racking as most of yours—I wouldn't trade my job and most of you wouldn't trade your jobs, as hard as they may be, for that of a good wife who supervises a family of children all day long, not to speak of a few other responsibilities that engage her time from morning to night. And I sometimes wonder whether or not we are playing fair. I don't have in mind clothes and money and precious gems. I learned a long time ago, as no doubt most men have discovered, that women are strange pieces of humanity. We like, figuratively speaking, meat that sticks to the ribs; they like salads. We enjoy big boxes of candy; they like dainty packages. We glory in competitive, bold heroics; they cherish the beautiful, sympathetic acts of devotion. We knew that once when we went a-courtin'. Is it possible that we have forgotten in later years?

I shall never forget two pictures that have forced themselves upon my mind.

The first occurred in an airplane in which I was riding some time ago. Near me sat a fine-looking gentleman and his devoted wife. They were well dressed, evidently had plenty of money, and both, I suspect, were well read. My attentions were drawn especially when I noticed that the wife placed her hand on his arm and begged him to refrain from some discourteous act that he insisted he would perform toward one of the stewardesses. Evidently the young woman had overlooked some wish that he had made earlier.

"I'm not going to stand for it any longer," he said. "That stewardess is going to get a piece of my mind, and I'm going to put her straight right now." His wife's eyes pleaded with him but he refused to listen to her pleas. Getting to his feet in the presence of those in the cabin, he made his way to the stewardess. It was only a little act, to him quite insignificant, but sufficient to bring color and apparent disappointment to the face of one whose smallest wish at one time he would have moved heaven and earth to grant.

The other picture was in the dining room of a beautiful home where I was staying on a weekend. Approaching the breakfast table, I noticed that a lovely fresh flower had been placed beside the wife's plate, a rose that I knew had been picked but a few moments before from their own garden. And as I looked at the husband, a stake president, and asked him why, he only smiled, but his eyes twinkled like those of a schoolboy who had found his first love. He was no sissy; rather, he was a man of real power in the community, successful in his profession, and as busy every day, it seemed to me, as a man could possibly be. Yet he found time each morning to remember with real devotion the wish of a woman's heart.

You know, men, we have always been told that it is impossible for us to understand women. But I am thinking it must be pretty hard also for the average wife to understand why a friend's husband will work so hard to give her the best of material things and then forget the tender courtesies that please her most.

Endeavor consciously to find new and better ways of doing ordinary things.

25

My Wife's Husband

There are some things that I wish my wife's husband would do! I admit that he's a very busy man, arising very early in the morning and conducting a multitude of business appointments almost every day throughout the week and often on long church assignments every weekend, as well as accepting many speaking assignments throughout the area.

But I wish my wife's husband would realize that all of this, hard as it sometimes appears, is no more tiresome and nerve-racking than superintending the dressing of several active children, preparing breakfast, getting those children off to school on time, playing servant to every ring of the doorbell, every collector who appears on the scene, every salesman—silently refusing many times in the day to answer the doorbell or telephone and then changing her mind and answering them for fear it may be a friend or stranger in need. Oh, it's a great life being a conscientious wife!

I wish my wife's husband could remember every evening when he comes home that no matter how hard he has labored, she has labored just as hard; no matter how weary and discouraged he may be with the way things have gone during the day, she has equal reason to be tired and discouraged with the load of her multitudinous and hectic responsibilities.

If my wife's husband could always realize this, I believe that he would try even harder than he does to forget his own troubles and to bring into his home a spirit of fun and optimism and assurance that would make every member of the family glad to be alive. One cannot lessen his good will toward a customer, a business associate, a student, or a neighbor by emphasizing the wrong that the other person might have done to him during the day. The more two tired people spread their ill feelings, the worse these feelings become. And it should be much easier for a husband to leave his troubles at the office, in the field, or in the car than it is for a wife to forget hers in the very spot where they happen during the day.

However, I do wish that he would more freely share with his wife some of the excitement and interest of his work. Ours is a partnership, and she should feel that she is a part of my work and my interests just as I, by the very nature of living in our home, am involved in her interests and activities. I wish he would remember that though she may be involved more in child care and homemaking responsibilities, she also has other interests and insights that may help me in my own work and that we can share together.

I wish my wife's husband were as careful in the home where she works as he is in his own office to get rid of the little but distracting annoyances. If a window in his office sticks, if a door fails to fit properly, if his pen refuses to function one hundred percent, if some little article that he needs in his office work is lost or broken, he proceeds at once to have the necessary corrections or repairs made, for he realizes how his work is hindered and how distracting it is to his nervous system when any little thing that he needs gets out of order.

But because he does not spend as much time in the house as she does, he is apt to let a leaky or thumping faucet go for several days before he does anything about it. A cranky washing machine, a wobbly ironing board, a screen door with just enough give to let in an occasional fly, a caster on one leg of the bed that doesn't quite turn right but must be moved every day, walls that need painting—such little things, but they grow into monstrosities before the day is over.

But say, gentlemen, there's no reason why I should blame myself any more than should some of you. I'd like to make a bargain with every husband reading this chapter. Suppose that for the rest of the week we refuse to correct any of the trivial annoyances that may occur in our work. If we drop our pen and bend the point, we just do the best we can with it in that condition for the rest of the week. If the saw that you carpenters use or the razor that you barbers use gets dull, don't take the time to sharpen it. Do the best you can under the circumstances.

No matter what our vocations may be, if we were to try such an experiment for a week, say—just long enough to feel its nerve-racking effects—I have an idea that the next week would see many improvements in the home offices where the good wives are doing their work, and why not? If two members of a partnership assume an equal share of the responsibility, is there any reason why our wives should not have a little proportion of the conveniences that rightly go with their work?

And I wish my wife's husband would remember more often some of the little things that make a sweetheart husband-wife relationship so special. I wish he would be more aware of the anniversaries and special days we share. I wish he would remember occasionally that courting doesn't end when a couple make their marriage vows—it just enters a deeper and more significant phase, when the little niceties and thoughtfulness that were so appreciated before marriage are appreciated even more.

I wish my wife's husband would make time, in his busy schedule, to take her to special places, to bring her flowers or other symbols of his love for her, to show more appreciation and gratitude for the little things she does for him and the entire family. Ours is an eternal union, and such attributes as thoughtfulness, kindness, consideration, gratitude, sharing, compassion, genuinely caring—all of these become more important each day we are together. May our love continue to grow because my wife's husband—and his wife—both find eternal joy in it.

Courtesy is a great lubricant.

26

My Husband's Wife

Conversely, if our wives were to write a chapter or response to the preceding, entitled "My Husband's Wife," perhaps this is what they might say:

As a wife, mother, and homemaker, my husband's wife wears many hats every day: meal planner and cook, seamstress, dishwasher, scrubwoman, laundress, baby sitter, teacher, shopper, budget-balancer, home secretary, counselor and confidante to children and husband of widely varied ages, interests, and problems.

But though she is sometimes so busy with all these daily responsibilities that by the time her husband comes home she just wants to collapse, I wish my husband's wife would take some time each day to think about what she might do to please him. Sometimes she takes her relationship with him so much for granted that she overlooks small things that could offer large satisfactions. Just planning one or two nice gestures for his arrival home could make the difference between an average evening and a special evening.

I wish that my husband's wife would learn to ask for his advice a little more often. She often finds it easy to give orders to him in the same manner in which she instructs the young children. She needs to remember that in the spirit of his masculinity, he will usually turn over heaven and earth to please her when he is approached in the right way rather than merely told what to do.

I wish that my husband's wife were more available when he invites her to do something with him. Of course there are children to be considered, the PTA, visiting teaching, homemaking, Church meetings, to mention only a few of her responsibilities, but she needs to remember that when he invites her to lunch or a business meeting or a social event that is important to him but seems a nuisance to her, he wouldn't have asked if he didn't really want her to accompany him. She needs to keep her schedule flexible enough to please him when he asks.

I wish that my husband's wife would remember to invite her breadwinner to go shopping with her once in a while. She needs to keep him informed of the price of clothing, food, and other household and family needs so he can appreciate that she really isn't a spendthrift with his hard-earned dollars.

I wish that my husband's wife would remember always to keep up her appearance. She knows he doesn't expect her to be a glamour girl, but she shouldn't forget that he also has a right to be proud to be with her wherever they go.

I wish that my husband's wife would remember to be affectionate throughout marriage. She needs to realize that she plays a great role in setting the tone of the marriage, and if she is sensitive to his needs and moods, she can smooth over many rough times just by her affection and her physical consideration.

And I wish that my husband's wife would remember to persuade, not provoke; to counsel, not command; to pray, not probe; to lead with love, not force through threats; to be feminine without sacrificing identity; and most of all, to be careful of the most important and precious person in her life—a husband who will do almost anything she wants him to do if she just loves him into it.

"And again, inasmuch as parents have children in Zion, or in any of her stakes which are organized, that teach them not to understand the doctrine of repentance, faith in Christ the Son of the living God, and of baptism and the gift of the Holy Ghost by the laying on of the hands, when eight years old, the sin be upon the heads of the parents."

—D&C 68:25

27

The Prodigal Parent

A certain child had two parents, and the younger of them, the mother, said to the child, "Daughter, give me the portion of your life that rightly belongs to me. Have I not borne you with much pain and tribulation? Have I not watched over you in time of sickness and of health? Now give me your respect, your love, and your obedience at home and when we are separated one from the other."

In response, the little girl cuddled close to her mother's heart and, with chubby arms wrapped tightly around her mother's neck, said, "I love you. I love you very much, and I promise to do anything that you want me to."

Then the mother, taking these priceless possessions of love and confidence into her heart, began to live in a world that was strangely different and far distant from the innocent, beautiful life of the child: wild drinking parties that sapped the strength and dulled the vision of better things; much seeking after guilt; a big display in the high esteem of reckless folk; a reckless search for thrills of every sort, on stage, on screen, in racy books, and in wild adventure with vulgar-minded folk. Then came the terrible awakening—a sense of futility, a realization of the lack of ability in the life that she had lived, and a longing for the simplicity of a former day.

And coming thus to herself, she said, "I will rise and go to my child"—not as a prodigal son would seek his father for food, not as the prodigal father would bid again for the fellowship of his son, but with the desire to help in a mother's way. She would say unto her child, who by this time had grown into young womanhood, "Daughter, I have sinned against heaven and in your sight; because of my neglect, I have proved myself unworthy to be called your mother. But I am repentant now; I have seen my terrible mistake, and I am willing to do anything in my power to make you what you should become."

But on the morrow, after the mother had repented of all her words to her daughter, the young woman replied, "Dear mother, I appreciate all that you have said, knowing how you have neglected me to my own hurt, and yet how anxious you are now to make amends. But your offer of help has come too late. When I was a child, I promised to respect your position of authority, and that I have done. Seeing the way in which you spent your time in the company of your reckless companions and the hours you spent away from home, I did what I thought you would have me do, and I followed your example in the company of my own friends, building into my life habits of thought and action that would be very difficult now to change, even if I had the desire. And now you come to me in your older days, asking one who is strong of body and enjoying every passing thrill to give up what you now consider to be trivial and not worth the while."

"But, daughter, I did not understand!"

"Nor have you taught me to understand," said the daughter. "Like parent, like child. You have had your fling; I am having mine, even as you yourself have taught me to do." And the daughter ordered no fatted calf nor did she put a simple ring upon her mother's hand; rather, she left a weight upon her heart. What the mother had once foolishly surrendered, she could not now take up again. What she had sung, in moments of wild revelry, now echoed back in a hollow, mocking laugh, the story of a mother who would mortgage the soul of an innocent child for the raucous appeal of the heartless world.

The words of the Lord echo so aptly in these latter days: "And again, inasmuch as parents have children in Zion, or in any of her stakes which are organized, that teach them not to understand the doctrine of repentance, faith in Christ the Son of the living God, and of baptism and the gift of the Holy Ghost by the laying on of hands, when eight years old, the sin be upon the head of the parents." (D&C 68:25.)

"Suffer little children . . . to come unto me: for of such is the kingdom of heaven."

—Matthew 19:14

28

And Then Some

Some time ago while traveling in the South Pacific, I was privileged to listen to a group of Primary children sing, and oh, how they could sing! Their voices, raised to the heavens, told of the great faith and love they have for the Lord.

It never seems to matter in what culture I find myself, the style of dress, or the language: the spirit is always the same. That same sweet spirit has prompted me to believe more readily those divine words of two thousand years ago: "Suffer little children . . . to come unto me: for of such is the kingdom of heaven." (Matthew 19:14.) Whether we are dealing with tiny tots or teenagers, the Lord has placed a great and awesome responsibility upon parents and teachers alike. Our commission is great, and our stewardship reminds me of a popular poem:

> Each is given a bag of tools,
> A shapeless mass and a book of rules;
> And each must make, ere life is flown,
> A stumblingblock or a steppingstone.
>
> —R. L. Sharp

The Prophet Joseph Smith felt that the power of introspection is one of the finest attributes we can acquire. He was able to find flaws in his own character and eradicate them. We need to apply this same test as parents and as teachers. We need to continually ask ourselves, What kind of a parent or teacher am I? Then we might ask, What kind of a worker does the Lord expect me to be?

I'd like to suggest some types of individuals that the Lord needs in this work today. You fill in the gaps and see where your life measures up.

Some time ago while presiding over the New England Mission, I used to ask my elders and sisters this question: "Have you caught the vision?" In other words, do you understand the real reasons for a mission? Now, could we ask ourselves today this same question? Have you caught the true vision of parenthood or the program in which you find yourself leading or teaching? Can you see through the mechanics of the day-to-day work? Can you stand apart from the pressures of programs and see how each part can touch the eternal spirit of a child of God? Will you stop for a moment to look at the whole program and realize that you are on an unbeatable team, the Lord's team? Have you learned that the program to which you have been assigned is a means to an end, and that people are more important than programs?

Many times in my life and travels I have seen firsthand the far-reaching effects of the programs of the Church as they appeal to children and help them to mature. I have seen countless parents join the Church because of a child or teenager who was active in one of our programs. This is the true vision, the Lord's program, and the result is young people who are trained in the way in which they should go and who will not depart from the truth.

I remember once hearing an eight-year-old child at a sacrament meeting who had been taught correct principles at home and at Primary. He said, "Do you know why I'm glad to be a Latter-day Saint?

"First of all, because my church teaches me that my Heavenly Father is an exalted man just as I will be some day. This makes it easy for me to pray to him and to understand him. My church teaches me that I am one of God's children, whether I am in California, Hawaii, or wherever I go; everyone I meet is my brother and sister. If all of God's children knew this simple truth, there would never be any wars.

"Just a few months ago I was baptized, and I am so glad my church has taught me that from now on I must watch everything I do and say, because I may never know when someone will judge the Church by me.

"In just four more years I can pass the sacrament of the Lord. This is a blessing that even the president of the United States or the prime minister or king of another country does not have.

"I'm so glad my church teaches me to pay tithing and fast offerings. This is the way I can help to build temples and colleges, and just as important, it teaches me never to be selfish.

"I am very proud of the missionaries of the Church. I hope that when I grow up I will be strong so that I will go whenever and wherever the Lord asks me to go."

We can be reasonably confident that this young man will grow up and weather the problems of life, for he is being taught by precept and example.

If we wish to be effective in touching and reaching young people, another important characteristic is our own commitment to gospel principles. In other words, example is the key. If we don't practice what we teach, our words to our children become "as sounding brass and a tinkling cymbal." If we are to be truly effective leaders, we must be committed to that which we believe and teach. It must be an operating power in our lives. Children see so quickly through hypocrisy and insincerity. Remember, it was the Savior who said, "But whoso shall offend one of these little ones which believe in me, it were better for him that a millstone were hanged about his neck, and that he were drowned in the depth of the sea." (Matthew 18:6.)

The Savior has outlined very explicitly our responsibilities as leaders of young people. We never want to be caught in the position of the man who approached a young boy who was fishing on the Sabbath and asked, "What does your father think of your fishing on Sunday?" The little lad replied, "I don't know; why don't you ask him? He's under the bridge digging worms."

I've always been grateful for a faithful teacher who taught me when I was young that "example sheds a genial ray that men are apt to borrow, so first improve yourself today, and then your friends tomorrow."

Commitment, combined with example, should be a foremost tool in the Lord's work.

One of the greatest truths believed in and taught by the Latter-day Saint is that we are the literal spirit children of a Heavenly Father. Inherent with this truth is the idea that we too have a God-like or divine potential. We should teach all of God's children from birth that they are his children, that he loves them and has placed them on earth to succeed. I believe that children should be imbued with the idea that through repentance and work they can someday become like God. There is a beautiful verse that expresses this thought.

> In the breast of a bulb is the promise of spring;
> In the little blue egg is the bird that will sing;
> In the heart of the seed is the hope of the sod;
> In the soul of a child is the kingdom of God.

Young people, and particularly children, must have love unconditionally. Did you ever wonder why animals or pets are so precious to the young? It's because an animal gives unconditional love—there are no questions or doubts. This is the kind of love that Christ taught—to hate the sin and not the sinner; to understand but not condone. When children become aware that we love them regardless of their mistakes, and that we put their happiness on a par with our own, then we will have come a long way toward making any program a divine instrument in the shaping of young lives.

Good or bad, quiet or noisy, receptive or aloof, happy or sad, each child should be loved unconditionally. This implies a need on our part for wisdom, restraint, and self-control.

A young mother once told me of her struggle for one of the most cherished of all trophies, the struggle for self-control, for self-composure and cheerful acceptance of things that cannot be changed. It seemed that this mother, herself a leader in the church, had worked long and hard to construct a dress from an unusually difficult pattern. It was nearly completed when she returned to it after a brief interruption to find that it had been hacked to ribbons with scissors by her two-year-old daughter. Then came the struggle that we all fight at crucial moments in our lives—for self-control. This fine woman emerged as a victor. She had lost a dress but she won a far more important battle. What power comes with self-control and love for others!

In teaching and trying to motivate individuals, I am convinced that a great key to such success is in seizing the teaching moment. I learned some years ago as a young teacher that I could get closer to a young person in one moment, sometimes in a cultural hall, at the drinking fountain, or in the parking lot, than by spending hours of formal teaching in the class. We must be alert for the opportunities to teach wherever and whenever we go.

I remember one occasion with my wife and several missionaries in New England, where we used to make it a practice to capture the teaching moment. One day after a zone conference we stopped at a nearby restaurant to eat. Several of the missionaries had been invited to join us. Our waitress, as she approached the table and saw so many young men, was obviously curious as to what sort of group this was. As she approached the table, I greeted her with this statement: "Well, ma'am, what do you think of my boys?"

She was visibly shocked. "They're all yours?" she inquired.

"Yes, ma'am," I replied. "And what's more, they are all ordained ministers."

Then I said, "Can you guess where they all come from?" She looked over the group in wonderment as I had each elder in turn tell where he was from. After she had taken our orders and had gone to place them, I challenged one of the elders to commit this waitress to listening to our discussion later that week. He did it very cleverly, and I'm pleased to indicate another convert was added to the ranks. How different it might have been had we not seized the opportunity or chance to teach!

Sometimes these teaching moments take a different twist. Some friends in California shared one of their family experiences with me. This father and his lovely wife have two small children. At the time Sandy was five years old, with blond hair and blue eyes, exuberant and full of life. Her long-awaited infant brother, Craig, had come from the hospital a few days before when he was just a week old. Sandy was obviously thrilled with the new addition. One day, however, Sandy misbehaved, and her mother justifiably corrected her. As five-year-olds will do, she pouted and then resolutely said, "I wish I had a new mama." Well, you can imagine how that would hurt you as a parent. But this faithful Latter-day Saint mother decided to capitalize on one of those teaching moments. She approached her daughter, placed her arm around her shoulders, and said, "Now, honey, you know that before we came to this earth we lived with Heavenly Father, and it is very possible that you might have chosen Daddy and me to be your parents."

Sandy got the message. It hit home. You see, the

situation had now been reversed; what if she had chosen them? She had no one to blame but herself.

The incident passed and so did a few days. Then one afternoon Craig started to cry. His sobs echoed from his crib throughout the house. Sandy's mother arrived at the bedroom door just in time to see Sandy approaching the crib, and she saw this scene and heard the ensuing conversation. Sandy placed her small hand on the bald head of her crying baby brother and said sympathetically, "It's too late now, Craig—you've already picked them."

This story illustrates that we are all teachers by nature. It shows that children are very perceptive and cling to ideas more readily than we imagine. Our goal should be to captivate that interest and teach them simple truths.

What is a teacher? He is a prophet. He lays the foundation of tomorrow. He is an artist. He works with the precious clay of unfolding personality.

The teacher is a friend. His heart responds to the faith and devotion of the students. He is a citizen. He is a selected individual and licensed for the improvement of society.

The teacher is an interpreter. Out of his mature and wider life, he seeks to guide the young. He works with higher and finer values of civilization.

The teacher is a builder. He is a culture bearer. He leads the way toward worthier tastes, saner attitudes, more gracious manners, higher intelligence.

The teacher is a planner. He sees the young lives before him as a system that shall grow strong in the light of truth.

The teacher is a pioneer. He is always attempting the impossible and winning out.

The teacher is a reformer. He seeks to remove the handicaps that weaken and destroy life.

The teacher is a believer. He has abiding faith in the improvability of the human race.

We should all take to our church work an enthusiastic spirit and a positive attitude. It was Ralph Waldo Emerson who said that nothing great was ever achieved without enthusiasm. I believe that. If we could infuse this principle into everything we did, into all of our work, we'd have greater results. Enthusiasm implies extra effort.

A retired business executive friend of mine was once asked the secret of his great success. He replied that it could be summed up in three words: "And then some." "I discovered at an early age," he said, "that most of the differences between average people and top people can be explained in these three words. The top people do what is expected of them—and then some. They are thoughtful and considerate of others—and then some. They meet their obligations and responsibilities fairly and squarely—and then some. They are good friends to their friends—and then some. They can be counted on in an emergency—and then some.

"And so it is when we do what is assigned to us in the church—and then some. Then the Lord pays in full—and then some."

Enthusiasm comes from the Greek words *en* and *theos.* These literally mean God in us. As Latter-day Saints we ought to be the happiest, most enthusiastic people in the world because of what we know concerning God's divine plan.

A young couple in New England were visitors in our home before and after they joined the Church. Since they joined the Church, they have become one of the most enthusiastic couples that I had ever met. The gospel has changed their lives, and they are deeply indebted. I have seen them stay after sacrament meeting for over an hour just discussing with their newfound friends the many facets of the gospel. They have truly caught a vision. I remember one afternoon when this lovely lady cornered one of my missionaries who had grown up in the Church and had been somewhat unenthusiastic about missionary work. She put her finger right under his nose and said, "Elder, I hope you realize how lucky you are to be a member of this church." Her enthusiasm changed the course of his whole mission.

I've often told missionaries wherever they are to put SPAM in their lives. I'm not referring to canned meat. This is the slogan we used to use in the mission field; it means a "Super Positive Attitude Mentally." It may sound unusual, but I think it's good. We need a Super Positive Attitude Mentally today, for there has never been a chance like this in the history of the world for so many to do so much. President David O. McKay once said that "next to eternal life, the most precious gift that our Heavenly Father can bestow upon men is his children." It reminds me, in conclusion, of this verse:

> I see a mind all new and unstained
> And a heart and a conscience untouched,
> And a body that holds an untouched soul
> Is given to me to be trained.
> Oh Lord, give me the strength to measure the mind
> And read what the intellect holds,
> To judge it aright, and develop its might
> Till its power completely unfolds.

"Ideals are like stars; you will not succeed in touching them with your hands. But like the seafaring man on the desert of waters, you choose them as your guides, and following them you will reach your destiny."

29

Developing a Philosophy of Life

1. Practice putting your whole soul into what you do.
2. Don't take yourself too seriously. Learn to see the humor in all things.
3. Search for the bright side of things that look dark.
4. Laugh at good stories and learn to tell them.
5. Cultivate amiability, graciousness, and adaptability. Conceal unpleasant feelings.
6. Force yourself to do things you should do but are afraid you cannot do.
7. Banish troubles quickly. Do not inflict them upon your friends.
8. Keep grievances to yourself when tempted to recite them to others.
9. Resist the temptation to become ruffled with chronic faultfinders.
10. Try consciously to keep your feelings in tune with the feelings of those about you.
11. Overcome the temptation to give way to anger. ". . . let not the sun go down upon your wrath." (Ephesians 4:26.)

12. Insist on some solitude. ". . . in quietness and in confidence shall be your strength." (Isaiah 30:15.)
13. Be willing to face facts of life squarely and frankly.
14. "Nothing is ever done beautifully that is done in rivalship, nor nobly which is done in pride." (Ruskin.)
15. Study your own mistakes to determine how they might have been avoided.
16. Study the personal qualities of effective leaders, and cultivate their friendship as far as possible.
17. Endeavor to overcome objectionable mannerisms.
18. When appearing before others, look them in the face.
19. Study the needs and interests of the group.
20. In group activities, endeavor to contribute more than you get.
21. Sacrifice, within reason, personal advantage when it stands clearly in the way of the welfare of the group.
22. Refrain from hurting the feelings of another person, no matter how little he is or how little you like him.
23. Put cooperation in place of competition.
24. Lead others to your view, if you are sure you are right, by questions rather than arbitrary statements or argumentation.
25. Do not disparage others, but help and encourage them instead.
26. Do not oppose the ideas of others, but substitute better ones instead.
27. In cases of disagreement, try to get and to consider sympathetically the other person's viewpoint.
28. Preserve an open mind on all debatable questions. Discuss, but don't argue. It is a mark of superior minds to disagree and yet be friendly. "However, some open minds should be closed for repairs."
29. Take for granted the friendliness of others. Don't wait for them to speak first.
30. Be easy to get along with.
31. Be kind. Nothing is so beautiful, no quality so irresistible.

32. Endeavor consciously to find new and better ways of doing ordinary things.
33. Watch for and seize upon opportunities to do favors unasked.
34. Study to do the little things that others like, and show your pleasure in doing them.
35. Go out of your way to cheer up folks.
36. Courtesy is a great lubricant.
37. Help others to get acquainted.
38. Never fail to keep promises and appointments.
39. Practice blindness to others' faults, looking always for their good qualities instead.
40. Keep skid chains on your tongue; always say less than you think. Cultivate a pleasing voice. How you say it often counts far more than what you say.
41. Suggest rather than command or demand.
42. Do not fail to give credit to the proper persons and sources.
43. Do committee work when possible. Good committee men are rare.
44. Don't be too anxious about getting just dues. Do your work, be patient, keep your disposition sweet, forget self, and you will be respected and rewarded.
45. Be interested in others—their pursuits, their welfare, their homes and families, their personal interests, habits, hobbies, the things they have done, the things they own, their knowledge and opinions, their names, the people and things they revere, their wants and needs. Take the trouble to exhibit your respect for their interests. Let everyone you meet, however humble, feel that you regard him as a person of importance.
46. "If we succeed without sacrifice, it is because someone else has sacrificed before us; if we sacrifice without succeeding, it may be that someone else will succeed after us."
47. "When I met him I was looking down. When I left

him I was looking up." (A Yankee definition of personality.)

48. "Lincoln was not great because he was born in a log cabin, but because he got out of it." (James Truslow Adams.)
49. "I do the very best I can, the very best I know how, and mean to keep on doing so until the end. If the end brings me out right what is said against me will not matter. If the end brings me out wrong, ten angels swearing I was right would make no difference." (Abraham Lincoln.)
50. "Ideals are like stars; you will not succeed in touching them with your hands. But like the seafaring man on the desert of waters, you choose them as your guides, and following them you will reach your destiny."

Be willing to face facts of life squarely and frankly.

30

Qualities of Life

In the first chapter, I challenged you to analyze your own philosophy of life to determine how you measured up in light of gospel standards. As we close, check yourself and then, in the weeks and months ahead, review for constant improvement. I challenge you to have—

1. A purpose in life.
2. Definiteness in decisions.
3. Unwavering courage.
4. A keen sense of justice.
5. Definiteness of plans.
6. Willingness to accept and enlist help.
7. A desire always to do more than assigned.
8. A pleasant personality.
9. Sympathy and understanding.
10. Mastery of detail.
11. Cooperation.
12. Loyalty.
13. Enthusiasm.
14. Perseverance. (A real leader never quits.)
15. A good sense of humor.

SELF-EVALUATION CHECKLIST

Place a check (√) in the appropriate column to the side of each quality. Be honest with yourself.

PERSONAL QUALITY	VERY STRONG	SUFFICIENT	NEED DEVELOPMENT
Agreeableness			
Agressiveness			
Ambition			
Concentration			
Cheerfulness			
Criticism (of others)			
Dependability			
Determination			
Enthusiasm			
Faith			
Friendliness			
Honesty			
Humor			
Insight			
Intelligence			
Initiative			
Ingenuity			
Keeping a confidence			
Loyalty			
Language (use of)			

Love of:			
People			
Places			
Life			
Gospel			
Manners			
Memory			
Modesty			
Neatness			
Observation			
Physical fitness			
Posture			
Patience			
Politeness			
Punctuality			
Perseverance			
Responsibleness			
Self-esteem			
Sociableness			
Sincerity			
Self-confidence			
Self-control			
Teachableness			
Truthfulness			
Tactfulness			
Unselfishness			

INDEX